P9-DFI-610

# STRAW BALE SOLUTIONS

**CREATIVE TIPS** FOR **GROWING VEGETABLES IN BALES**

AT HOME IN COMMUNITY GARDENS AND AROUND THE WORLD

JOEL KARSTEN

COOL SPRINGS PRESS

# Dedication

This book is dedicated to my greatest friend, my teacher, and my father—
all the same man. Your influence is immeasurable and everlasting.

Brimming with creative inspiration, how-to projects, and useful information to enrich your everyday life, Quarto Knows is a favorite destination for those pursuing their interests and passions. Visit our site and dig deeper with our books into your area of interest: Quarto Creates, Quarto Cooks, Quarto Homes, Quarto Lives, Quarto Drives, Quarto Explores, Quarto Gifts, or Quarto Kids.

© 2018 Quarto Publishing Group USA Inc. Text © 2018 Joel Karsten

First published in 2018 by Cool Springs Press, an imprint of The Quarto Group,
401 Second Avenue North, Suite 310, Minneapolis, MN 55401 USA.
T (612) 344-8100 F (612) 344-8692 www.QuartoKnows.com

All rights reserved. No part of this book may be reproduced in any form without written permission of the copyright owners. All images in this book have been reproduced with the knowledge and prior consent of the artists concerned, and no responsibility is accepted by producer, publisher, or printer for any infringement of copyright or otherwise, arising from the contents of this publication. Every effort has been made to ensure that credits accurately comply with information supplied. We apologize for any inaccuracies that may have occurred and will resolve inaccurate or missing information in a subsequent reprinting of the book.

Cool Springs Press titles are also available at discount for retail, wholesale, promotional, and bulk purchase. For details, contact the Special Sales Manager by email at specialsales@quarto.com or by mail at The Quarto Group, Attn: Special Sales Manager, 401 Second Avenue North, Suite 310, Minneapolis, MN 55401 USA.

10 9 8 7 6 5 4 3 2 1

ISBN: 978-0-7603-5739-2

Library of Congress Cataloging-in-Publication Data

Names: Karsten, Joel, 1969– author.
Title: Straw bale solutions / Joel Karsten.
Description: Minneapolis, MN : Cool Springs Press, 2018. | Includes index.
Identifiers: LCCN 2017048982 | ISBN 9780760357392 (sc)
Subjects: LCSH: Vegetable gardening. | Raised bed gardening. | Straw—Utilization.
Classification: LCC SB321 .K28 2018 | DDC 635—dc23
LC record available at https://lccn.loc.gov/2017048982

Acquiring Editor: Mark Johanson
Project Manager: Alyssa Bluhm
Art Direction and Cover Design: Cindy Samargia Laun
Interior Design and Layout: Wendy Holdman
Editorial Assistance: Jennifer Ebeling

Printed in China

STRAW BALE GARDENS® is a registered trademark of Joel Karsten, and references the specific method of gardening developed by Karsten, and products related to this specific method of gardening.

# CONTENTS

# CHAPTER 1

# THE STRAW BALE GARDENS STORY

A DECADE AGO, no one had heard of Straw Bale Gardening. Today, more than half a million people all around the globe are growing vegetables in straw, often in climates and areas where a vegetable garden was never an option. And with so many Straw Bale Gardeners adapting the process to their own situations, you could say that there are half a million lessons to be learned about this new garden technology. *Straw Bale Solutions* is a testament to that.

The problem with pioneering a big new idea is that you don't really know you're doing it when you first begin. Nobody ever tells you, "That was a great idea you had the other day; you should keep doing this because it is obviously something that will really catch on in 20 years." You pursue the idea not because others are already doing it but because, to you, the idea makes sense in some way, and you believe it just might work.

Everyone has heard the old saying "Necessity is the mother of invention." In my case, it is absolutely true. I found myself a few years out of college, having purchased my first house and wanting to plant a garden. The problem I discovered was that the soil surrounding the house was terrible, with an average of 1 inch of topsoil and compacted gravel and clay underneath. I had a fancy new bachelor's degree in horticulture and nowhere to grow much of anything on my new property. About $200 would have likely been enough to build a couple of raised garden beds, but I'd need to fill them with compost—another $200. With a brand-new mortgage payment, a hefty student-loan payment, and a new business, I didn't have two nickels, not to mention $400. I did, however, have an idea!

Finding creative solutions to challenges is key to any gardening effort, but it is especially true with a relatively new method like Straw Bale Gardening. The contraption seen here is something I dreamed up to press planting bales from compost, helping to solve the problem of scarcity of straw. It works, but I did have the advantage of a fully stocked building center just down the street. When I see the truly resourceful solutions SBGers all over the world—many of them in extremely remote and disadvantaged conditions—have lit upon, I find it inspiring, and humbling too. I have learned so much from these amazing folks.

The Straw Bale Gardens story begins with a baling wagon on a small Minnesota farm many years ago.

As a kid, riding on a baling rack was something we did for much of each summer. I baled straw and hay for my dad and for many neighbors as well. It was common to end up with a busted bale that would get tossed out of the way against the barn. After a few months, or maybe by the following spring, those bales would often sprout and grow a rogue thistle or ragweed. It never failed that the biggest, tallest, greenest, and healthiest weeds on the farm were those that grew out of those decomposing bales. It would later be my job to toss those rotting old bales into the manure spreader, and I would notice up close how well things grew, as well as how wet and crumbly the bales were after they had lain by the barn for a year. It was this experience, tucked away somewhere in my head, that was the impetus of the bale-gardening idea 10 years later.

Why not use a few bales of decomposing straw to grow vegetables? If they were such good hosts for thistles and other weeds, shouldn't they grow peppers and tomatoes just as well? We had used straw to cover potatoes and to mulch many of our plants in our gardens on the farm, and the plants grew well surrounded by straw. If it didn't work, what was I out? I'd only be wasting few bales of straw I could get for little or nothing from the farm anyway.

I chased down a few of my old professors at the Saint Paul campus of the University of Minnesota and asked them if they thought I could successfully grow vegetables in bales of straw. They weren't very encouraging. They suggested I break the bales open and mix them into a compost for a season and then use the compost as a growing medium, but they didn't think the vegetables would get enough moisture or nutrients nor stay upright when the first stiff wind came along. I asked if they had ever tried growing anything in a rotting bale, and they all shrugged and said, "Let us know how it goes." I was referred to another horticulture professor at Texas A&M, who referred me to a professor at the University of Georgia, and he suggested I call up to Penn State. Then the professor at Penn State said the University of Minnesota would probably be a great resource.

Having learned nothing from academia, I called my dad. I explained that I wanted to try to grow a few peppers and tomatoes in some decomposing straw bales, like the bales that used to lie by the barn and sprout with weeds. I told him I had spoken to a few of my old professors and that none were very positive about the concept, and I asked what he thought. He said, "Well, I'm certainly not a professor—I'm just an old farmer—but what are you out if it doesn't work? You're only out a few old bales of straw."

He was right, but the embarrassment of trying to grow a garden in a new neighborhood and failing in full public view was a bit of a risk to my ego. My dad suggested I come to the farm the next weekend, and he would help me set up a garden with a few bales to try it. This began the grand experiment more than 20 years ago, and it didn't take long to realize how well it worked. The second season, I had bales tucked in my backyard, and I recruited a few others to try it over the next 10 years. Neighbors, friends, and a few other strangers showed some interest back then, but the concept of Straw Bale Gardening really didn't spread much until around 2007, when a local TV reporter showed some interest. The NBC reporter came to my house and shot video for a short human-interest story, and as he walked out the door, he suggested, "Joel, you know you should write a book about this method of gardening you've developed." He was the first to ever plant that seed in my head, and it sprouted quickly. I first had to convince myself this really was something that people were interested in knowing about. Then I had to attempt to write a book.

I had already created a three-page handout detailing the method I was using to prepare the bales. This black-and-white handout had a few suggestions about how to plant and what to grow, and it likely had a few spelling and grammatical errors as well. I decided to start with that handout, add a few pictures of my earliest gardens, and have my wife fix it up a bit so everything was spelled correctly and made sense. We designed a simple cover and formatted the whole thing into a 60-page booklet. It could easily be copied and have the pages folded, and it was bound with staples down the middle.

Soon after, a young woman emailed me and suggested that I make a page about Straw Bale Gardening on "the Facebook." After I figured out what Facebook was, with her help, I made a page and even put up a few pictures. I offered to mail out a copy of the "Learn to Grow a Straw Bale Garden" booklet to anyone who was interested in the technique. I charged a small fee to cover the copying costs and postage, and before long, I was spending 3 hours a day sending out booklets to people all over the world. These people would return to my Facebook page and post pictures of their beautiful vegetable gardens growing in bales. The pictures told the story, and people were starting to admit this crazy idea wasn't so crazy—it actually worked. Those who adopted the method early on would comment on what I already knew: how easy it was, that it involved almost zero weeding, and how they didn't have to bend over nearly as much as in traditional gardening. I had started using bales myself for two distinct reasons. First, I had only 1 inch of topsoil on my property, and second, I had no money to build raised beds. Now others were explaining to me all the reasons they had for turning to bales to solve their gardening problems, and I was learning more from them at that point than they were learning from me.

> "It's likely that if I would have had $400 to build those raised beds, none of you would have ever heard of me, and you certainly wouldn't be reading this book."

I sold those little self-published booklets to tens of thousands of gardeners all over the world over the next few years. People were growing beautiful vegetable gardens in bales in places where most folks don't think about gardening, from north of the Arctic circle in Alaska, Canada, and Norway, where the bales' warmth during decomposition gave them a huge head start on their normal growing season, to Israel, Egypt, Abu Dhabi, and Dubai, where there is no soil to speak of except sand. I started to see beautiful gardens growing

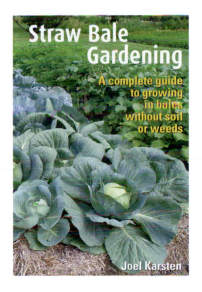

*Above:* My first "literary" effort was this 60-page booklet that I self-published. It was not fancy, but it got the information out, and I sold tens of thousands of them.

*Opposite:* Straw bales have basically zero nutritive value. So, why would plants grow in them? This was a key question.

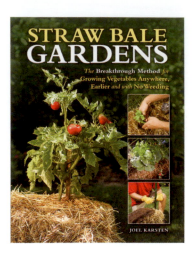

The first edition of *Straw Bale Gardens* came out in 2012 and quickly became one of the top three bestselling garden books in the United States.

in bales. I would get letters from people telling me about their knee-replacement surgery and how their Straw Bale Garden had allowed them to continue gardening. Other letters arrived from wheelchair users who had taken up gardening in bales, which were "exactly the right height and the right price." Several seasoned gardeners also wrote, including Gladys, a woman in her late 80s who told me how happy she was to be back in the garden again since her traditional garden had become too much for her 10 years earlier. The last line of her letter said, "I just had to write to you to let you know that you made at least one old lady really happy." Hundreds of letters from Straw Bale Gardeners around the world thanked me for introducing them to the concept . . . this certainly had gone far beyond any expectations I had ever dreamed of.

I wrote *Straw Bale Gardens,* my first "real" book, in 2012. It was published by Cool Springs Press and launched on March 15, 2013. Only 6 days later, on March 21, I got really lucky. The book received a full-page book review in a little East Coast newspaper; the writer called the technique revolutionary, and he raved about how gardeners he had interviewed loved the Straw Bale Gardens method. That "little" newspaper, the *New York Times*, also has good distribution and readership overseas, so the book was translated very quickly into several foreign languages and became an international best-seller among gardening books. The book was awarded the Pierre-Joseph Redouté award, a French book award for the best book of practical horticulture for 2014. In addition, a young landscape architect from France named Pascale Marq created an exhibition garden for the 2013 International Garden Festival at Chaumont in France's Loire Valley. For 6 months, from April to September in 2013, over 500,000 people, including some of the world's most influential gardening enthusiasts, toured the display gardens at Chaumont-sur-Loire and had a chance to see firsthand the Straw Bale Gardens technique in full production. (Read more in the profile of Pascale Marq on page 112.) It was a major coup for Straw Bale Gardening and helped the method gain acceptance and recognition all over the world. Many hundreds of articles were written after the first "real book" launched. For many readers, this was their first introduction to the technique. As with anything new, the skeptics abounded, and they have been out in force since day 1. The problem for them is that the evidence has clearly shown their skepticism is unwarranted. It is difficult to convince someone looking at pictures of a beautiful, productive, and healthy vegetable garden growing in bales that it doesn't work. I used to think it was my job to convince people that Straw Bale Gardening really works, but I've stopped doing that. I let people be convinced by others nowadays, and I won't argue with the skeptics like I used to; it takes too much effort and energy. Most of the time, the skeptic doesn't really understand the technique, and once they take the time to learn, they are quickly converted.

I made it on TV a few times early on, usually because people who knew reporters at the local TV stations were bragging constantly about their bale gardens. In an effort to keep them quiet, they would call the "Straw Bale Gardening guy," and my phone would ring. Reporters would come see my garden or I would send them pictures, and they were always astounded. Many TV reporters, radio hosts, and gardening writers I've spoken to over the years have become full-fledged practitioners of the Straw Bale Gardens method. Nobody is a better example than Cindy Hoedel, the garden writer for the *Kansas City Star* newspaper. She will admit that she was a bit skeptical the first time she interviewed me, but now she has become a huge fan of the method and writes a few articles each year about her own Straw Bale Garden, which I understand has grown exponentially. I love it when people are convinced by their own experience or by seeing a neighbor or a friend have success.

I've been asked over the years why I think Straw Bale Gardening has caught on. I could give a long list of all the benefits of using the Straw Bale Gardens method over planting a traditional garden in the soil, but that really doesn't answer the question. The real reason it has spread so quickly is that this method of gardening is conspicuous, in your face, and impossible to hide. Every neighbor within two blocks can see the rows of bales lined up in their neighbor's yard. They see their neighbor watering bales, later planting tomatoes in them, and then harvesting their crops sooner than anyone with traditional gardens. Their curiosity drives them to discover more. "How does this work?," "What are you growing?," and "How can I learn how to do this?" are common questions every new Straw Bale Gardener gets. Every person who plants a Straw Bale Garden becomes a teacher, like it or not, and they will be asked questions by curious friends or neighbors and begin teaching the basics. I joke with folks that for about 2 or 3 years they'll be a teacher, and then once they've been convinced that this really does work and they'll never go back to planting any other way, they will transition from teacher to preacher. Before long, they will find themselves telling people in the waiting room at the dentist's office about their bale garden and encouraging others to try it for themselves.

I've been speaking in public since I was in 4-H as a 10-year-old kid, always doing my county-fair radio interview with Mr. Bruce Lease, the voice of KWOA radio in my hometown. He knew my dad well and loved anyone who knew how to tell a story, and, like my dad, I knew how to tell a story. It might have been a story about one of the pigs or cows I was exhibiting at the fair or my tips about how to win at one of the carnival games on the midway. He never

This elaborate Straw Bale Garden was included in a famous garden festival in France's Loire Valley in 2013. It helped launch Straw Bale Gardens internationally.

knew what he would get, but I was getting a free T-shirt, so I was going to be on the radio one way or another.

In high school, I was president of Future Farmers of America (FFA) and quickly became comfortable speaking in front of groups of people. I enjoy public speaking today, especially when I am presenting a subject I am passionate about. There is nothing better than seeing the lights go on in people's heads once they first begin to understand exactly what Straw Bale Gardening is all about. By now, many people have heard the term "Straw Bale Gardening," but most really don't have a good grasp of the true benefits and impact. I love to be the one who opens up their minds and plants a brand-new idea, and I like to do it in a way they won't easily forget.

These days I spend much of my time traveling, giving presentations about the Straw Bale Gardens method. I have given my basic presentation more than 1,100 times since I planted that first garden via seminars, classes, speeches, interviews, podcasts, home and garden shows, grand openings, spring flings, and fall festivals all over the United States and around the world. To every person who hires me as a speaker, I promise three things for their important audience: 1) they will learn something they can implement and benefit from right away, 2) they will be entertained and share a few laughs at the stories they will hear, and 3) when they leave, it will be with a new appreciation for how anyone with a great idea can find success, and they will feel encouraged to pursue their own passions no matter how unlikely their success may seem.

I spent a little more than the first decade after starting my first Straw Bale Garden learning what really worked best in my gardens and developing a standard method for ensuring success for growers in any climate. I discovered this method works well using straw, hay, grass, or any kind of finely textured plant material once it is compressed tightly into a bale. I researched the best techniques for making these homemade bales for my second book, *Straw Bale Gardens Complete,* which was published in 2015. Once the method was refined, I applied for a federal trademark to represent the specific technique. It is now officially known as the STRAW BALE GARDENS® method.

I encourage others to research new adaptations and uses for the basic method I've developed and to share their results with me and with the world. As you will see later in this book, there are many examples of how others around the world have been able to utilize the Straw Bale Gardens method to solve their unique gardening problems. Difficulties that may have kept them from growing productive gardens in the past are now conquered with bales, allowing them to have productive gardens for the first time.

For me, gardening is a wonderful hobby. I love the flavor of fresh vegetables harvested moments before they land on my dinner plate. I love to be able to share what I grow with neighbors, friends, and family and donate to food shelves or others who are less fortunate. I spend a few bucks every spring buying bales, getting supplies, ordering exciting new seed varieties, and picking up a few flats of bedding plants to give my garden a jump-start. With that said, if everything I planted died, I would be still be okay. I'd simply run out to the market and buy the fruits and vegetables I need. I would be sad, but I wouldn't be hungry.

As I have traveled and met with leaders around the world in the "food security" landscape, I've become aware that for many people, things are not so simple. For many of the poorest populations around the world, if their crops fail, their existence and survival could be in question. It has become clear how many governments maintain their position of power over their populations by controlling food supplies.

When I was in Cambodia last year, an old man asked me, "What is the longest period of time you have ever gone without eating a meal?" I had to give it some serious thought, and to the best of my recollection, it was about 30 hours, before a medical procedure. I remember thinking how hungry I was, and food was the only thing I could think about for several hours before and after the procedure. Imagine if this were a daily or weekly reality, which it truly is for much of the world's poorer populations. The worst may not even be personal hunger but seeing your child go without food. In the wealthiest nations of the world, we may wonder why some populations lag behind in education and innovation, but it is easy to understand once you realize how hunger plays a role. Being hungry and constantly concerned about if, when, and from where your next meal will come can prevent anyone from focusing on teaching and learning.

"Hunger is the worst of all diseases" is a famous old quote by Max Muller, and I would have to agree. I hope you will agree that one of the greatest achievements of the worldwide spread of the Straw Bale Gardens method is the use of bales to grow crops in places around the world where gardens weren't previously possible. You'll read about a few examples later in this book. My hope is to write a future book featuring only examples of gardeners and farmers in developing countries who are using the Straw Bale Gardening technique to change their countries' crop production paradigm and solve the food-security problems in their own neighborhoods, villages, and cities. Solving hunger by sending food to governments and allowing them to distribute that food will never really solve the problem; it is only by teaching the people to feed themselves without government help that we will ever truly solve the problem of hunger in the world.

—Joel Karsten

*Above:* The original *Straw Bale Gardens* book has been translated into over 10 languages, and there are Straw Bale Gardens on every continent—including Antarctica. In fact, I almost called my new book *Straw Bale Planet*. It has been an amazing and humbling experience full of fascinating people, and the fun really is just beginning.

*Opposite:* You'll have to admit: Putting a bunch of straw bales in your yard and growing plants in them attracts some attention. To be honest, the curiosity it generates is one of the reasons Straw Bales Gardening has caught on so fast.

# CHAPTER 2

# THE STRAW BALE GARDENS METHOD

## The Secret to Straw Bale Gardening: You're Not Growing in Straw

IN MASTERING THE FUNDAMENTALS of the Straw Bale Gardens method, it is important to understand that nothing actually grows in straw.

Mind blowing, right?

At first glance, it may appear that Straw Bale Gardeners are planting vegetables in straw, but they are not—they are planting in *recently decomposed* straw.

Think about the most successful gardeners you know (even if they've never heard of Straw Bale Gardening), and more than likely, the number-one thing they all do is compost. Great gardeners understand the importance of compost and what compost provides to a garden. When it comes to Straw Bale Gardening, what is really happening is that the inside of the straw bale is turning into fresh compost.

If you think about anything that's ever been alive on planet Earth, everything you've ever seen that's alive—including us—eventually is decomposed by bacteria and turned back into soil. What is soil? It's a substrate that contains molecules of nitrogen, phosphorus, potassium—elemental materials that can then be reabsorbed through roots to form a new plant.

I always give the example of an old pine tree. After 100 years, a pine tree falls over on the forest floor and decomposes. Bacteria break the pine tree down into molecules, and suddenly up comes a flower. Or maybe a gardener gathers that soil and uses it to grow tomatoes. The plant decomposes into the soil. The following year, using the same molecules used to make the tomato, a pepper plant grows. You can't destroy matter; all you do is change its shape. Matter returns back to molecular form, and those same molecules create something else. It's an amazing thing that happens. These examples are a terrific way for people to understand that Mother Nature has been using the same molecules to rebuild living things over and over and over again for billions of years.

*Opposite:* Vegetables are easy to grow successfully in straw bales, but there are some very specific guidelines Straw Bale Gardeners need to follow to make it work.

Think about how important bacteria or other microbes are to growing plants. They are tiny little things that you can't even see with the naked eye, but they are doing the vast majority of the work of enabling these same molecules to be reused over and over. It's the basic biology behind Straw Bale Gardening that makes it work so well. I find it fascinating.

## The Science of Conditioning

Before planting in the bale, the straw must be conditioned for 2 weeks. *Conditioning* is just a fancy word for composting the straw in the center of the bale. The objective is to create the perfect environment for bacteria, fungi, mold, insects, and worms inside the bales.

The process of conditioning includes:

1. Soaking the straw stalks with water and adding nitrogen.

2. Moisture and nitrogen interacting with the straw, kicking decomposition into high gear.

3. Living organisms such as bacteria, fungi, mold, insects, and worms attacking, metabolizing, and digesting the straw, slowly turning it into soil.

(To properly condition your bales, follow the chart below.)

## At-a-Glance Conditioning Summary Chart

All volumes and quantities are per bale

| DAY IN PROCESS | TRADITIONAL FERTILIZER | ORGANIC FERTILIZER | WATER |
|---|---|---|---|
| Day 1 | ½ cup | 3 cups | Water to saturation |
| Day 2 | Skip | Skip | Water to saturation |
| Day 3 | ½ cup | 3 cups | Water to wash in fertilizer |
| Day 4 | Skip | Skip | Water to saturation |
| Day 5 | ½ cup | 3 cups | Water (warm is best) |
| Day 6 | Skip | Skip | Water (warm is best) |
| Day 7 | ¼ cup | 1 ½ cups | Water (warm is best) |
| Day 8 | ¼ cup | 1 ½ cups | Water (warm is best) |
| Day 9 | ¼ cup | 1 ½ cups | Water (warm is best) |
| Day 10 | 1 cup 10-10-10 | 3 cups with P and K | Water to wash in fertilizer |
| Day 11 | Skip | Skip | Keep moist until planting |
| Day 12 | Plant today | Wait 5 more days | Water any new plantings |

Much of this process would occur naturally, but we accelerate the process by feeding the bacteria to get it to quickly and completely colonize the bale. This also speeds the decomposition of the bale.

If you look through a microscope instead of just through your own eyes, the world looks very different. If you could look inside a straw bale during the conditioning process using a 400×-power microscope, you could watch the bacteria start to colonize the bale. Once the conditioning process starts with the addition of water and nitrogen, an amazing process is set in motion. The bacteria grow very rapidly thanks to the ample food supply of nitrogen. Nitrogen can be added through many sources, including organic blood meal, feather meal, or even simple lawn fertilizer (if you're not an organic gardener). Note that organic proteins require a longer time to work than refined manufactured fertilizers. This is because proteins must be processed by special bacteria in order to become a nitrogen derivative suitable for breaking down. If regular lawn fertilizer is used, the process begins immediately, and the bacteria multiply rapidly.

Essentially, there are only two things the bacteria need to begin their growth production: water and nitrogen. Once those prerequisites are satisfied, warmer air temperatures—something above 45° or 50°F—will cause these bacteria to start to multiply very rapidly.

## Ions: Recycling for Eons

Remember your high-school science class? No doubt the syllabus included the law of conservation of mass: "In any closed system, the amount of mass will remain constant over time. This means that matter can be neither created nor destroyed."

The law of conservation of mass works brilliantly in the garden. Take, for example, the decomposition of a stalk of wheat. Visibly, the stalk gradually turns from golden to black. On a microscopic level, the plant cells are breaking into molecules, and in turn, the molecules are shattering into ions. When it comes to plants, the mass of that plant, the plant ions, are never destroyed; they simply change shape, recombine, and get recycled into a new plant.

The periodic table is the master list of ions or elements. In plants, elements are tremendously important. In fact, in fertilizer, the levels of nitrogen (N), phosphorus (P), and potassium (K) are so important that the percentage of each is listed right on the package. Additionally, calcium, magnesium, sulfur, boron, chlorine, copper, manganese, molybdenum, and zinc are all building blocks for plant life.

During decomposition, the straw molecules break into ions, creating virgin "soil" (actually, compost) inside the bale. Waiting to be called back into service in the garden, the ions will be absorbed through the root tissue of the new plant growing in the bale. This is how the same ions that were inside the cells of a wheat stem last

High-nitrogen fertilizer stimulates the bacteria and fungi that are latent in the bales and causes them to accelerate the decomposition process, magically transforming straw into compost in just a couple of weeks.

The rapid reproduction and colonization of bacteria, vibrating and dividing in very large numbers inside of each bale, is exothermic. The heat generated makes the bale hospitable to plants days or weeks earlier than the soil surrounding the bales.

year are now inside the cells of a tomato this year. This recycling process has been happening for billions of years. The same charged particles have been used by different organisms over and over and over, growing and decomposing and growing and decomposing. We didn't invent recycling at all; nature has been recycling the same ions for eons.

## Inside the Bale: A World of Rapid Growth

In terms of teaching people how to Straw Bale Garden, there's one question that people ask most often: "Why do the straw bales get hot?"

This is the point where I begin to explain the science behind Straw Bale Gardening. Some people are fascinated by it, while others don't really care to know the specifics. For others, learning the science may be a foot in the door to understanding a biology that wasn't top of mind until they began to condition straw bales. It's truly a fascinating part of the biology of all life and how it works.

In order to reproduce, bacteria do not lay eggs or have babies; they simply split themselves in half. One splits into two, two become four, four become eight, and so on. In fact, you can actually see bacteria grow under a microscope. Under magnification, bacteria look like snakes or worms. When they get to a certain length, they pinch in half in the middle and then vibrate a little bit. The vibration happens right before each bacterium breaks apart and becomes two bacteria. The vibration causes friction that causes heat (scientifically, the vibration dissipates the energy as heat). These cells are microscopic, so the amount of heat from one bacterium vibrating is almost immeasurable. Once split in half, each of those two new halves begins to grow.

The newly formed bacteria will grow quickly and be ready to split, reproducing again, in as little as 15 minutes. Fifteen minutes later, each of those halves divides in half again. In a good growing environment, like the inside of a watered, fertilized bale in the spring, the bacteria will have food, water, and warm (60° to 90°F) temperatures and will grow quickly. Bacteria cells are small; a 400× microscope will allow you to only begin to see them, and individual cells don't take up much space. They will quickly colonize the entire bale because of their rapid growth rate.

## How Many Bacteria Does It Take to Heat up a Bale?

If a bale started with a single bacterium cell today and that cell and every new cell divided in half every 15 minutes for one entire day, how many bacterium cells would be alive in the bale at the same time the following day?

In 24 hours, you go from one bacterium to hundreds of trillions of bacteria, a really, really big number. I did the math, and it is unbelievable but true. In a single day, one bacterium will have produced 79,000,000,000,000,000,000,000,000,000 offspring.

(For those of you who are curious, here's the calculation: 24 hours = 96 15-minute cycles. Multiply $2 \times 2 \times 2$ 96 times, or calculate 2 to the power of 96.)

Each time one of those little bacteria divides in half and creates friction, it gives off a tiny amount of heat. A tiny amount of anything combined together 79 octillion times makes a lot of whatever that something was, so the tiniest amount of heat from one vibrating, shaking, wiggling bacteria, multiplied by 79 octillion, can easily heat the bales up to 125° to 150°F. In fact, Straw Bale Gardeners test their bales for heat to know when the bale is ready for planting. When they stick their hand in the middle the bale and it's 150°F in there, it feels hot.

## Joel Says

Why do we have refrigerators in our homes? Refrigerators keep food cold enough to prevent bacteria from growing on or in the food and causing it to decompose (spoil). Since a refrigerator is usually around 34°F, it should be noted that trying to grow bacteria in a bale while the outdoor temperatures are 34°F or colder isn't going to work. Wait for a warm day to begin conditioning the bales. I suggest starting no earlier than 20 days before your ZIP code's average last frost date. Usually you'll get at least 50°F daytime temps by then, and bacteria will begin to grow at 50°F. If extra heat is needed to get the bales cooking, cover them up with black plastic for a few sunny days, which will jump-start the bacteria growth.

## Straw on the Outside, Compost on the Inside

Even when completely conditioned and ready to plant, your bales may appear unchanged to the naked eye or look a little discolored or feel a little slimy on the inside. If you were to look inside the bale with a microscope, however, you would find a few hundred nonillion (that's 30 zeros, if you're curious) bacteria accumulated in the bale. If the bales have warmed up, they are likely colonized by lots of bacterium cells, and soon those bacteria will begin decomposing the straw and turning it into compost.

## Joel Says

Here's a real-world example most people can understand. Say you mow your lawn and forget your grass clippings in the bagger. Ten days later, when you reach your hand in the bagger to get your grass clippings out, it's warm and stinky and smelly and black—that's bacteria at work. It's usually bacilli, which are mostly just decomposers and harmless to humans. The bacteria are simply doing the job that Mother Nature gave them: to decompose organic material and turn everything into soil.

If you are planting seeds in your straw bales, you should first add a bed of potting soil (not dirt from your yard) on top. The soil's function is not to nourish the seed so much as it is to keep it from migrating too deeply into the bale.

## Planting in Warm Bales

Bales are usually ready to plant 12 days after the conditioning process has started. Organic nitrogen bales should be allowed 18 days to condition prior to planting. Keep the bales moist every day during the conditioning process, but do not use more than a gallon of water per bale per day. Air-temperature water, or water from the hose warmed overnight in a bucket, works much better than cold water directly from a garden hose. Bacteria like warm temperatures to reproduce.

Seedlings do not require a bed of potting soil. Just cut a hole in the top of the bale and plant seedlings as if you were transplanting them into your soil garden.

## Joel Says

The next time you see a compost pile steaming hot, imagine all those vibrating bacteria inside that pile, shaking and wiggling, generating so much friction that they are able to generate steam. A compost heater is a real thing. A large compost pile has pipes running through the pile. Water goes through the pipes and gets heated by the compost. The heated water is piped to a radiator in the house for heat extraction. Compost piles can get very hot, and if piled high enough, the compression of a giant pile of hay can create enough concentrated friction to spark a fire.

For up to 6 weeks after the conditioning process starts, the bales will be warmer than air temperatures. This phenomenon is great for the roots of young plants. When soil may still be 50°F on planting day early in the spring, the bale could be as warm as 100°F on the very same day. Young vegetable seeds sprout, establish roots, and grow quickly in a warm bale. Most plants get a big jump-start on the growing season because of this amazing warming phenomenon. Check the temperature inside the bales to make sure they are under 105°F before you transplant into them. To transplant, make a hole in the bale or, if it is too tight, use pliers to pull out a little straw to make a hole, and then drop the transplant into the planting hole. If seeds are being used, the temperature doesn't matter. Just apply a thin layer of planting mix or potting mix to hold tiny seeds in place and keep them moist until they germinate. Big seeds, such as peas and beans, seem to germinate well even if they are just pushed down 2 to 3 inches into the bale. *Never* use a shovel of soil from your garden on top of the bales. Adding garden soil to your bales introduces weed seeds, diseases, and insects.

## The Best Kinds of Bales

Bales may be composed of oat, wheat, rye, barley, or rice straw. They can also be made of any variety of grass or alfalfa hay. Use whatever is least expensive and readily available nearby. It is easy to make homemade bales (see the book *Straw Bale Gardens Complete*) using any mixture of leaves, grass clippings, trimmings, spent flowers, lake weeds, river grass, finely shredded branches, or leaves from any green plant within arm's reach in the landscape. Finely textured plants work best. What bales are made of isn't an important factor; once they decompose, they will support new plant growth. Keep in mind that all living cells eventually decompose and become ions. Ions are then used again to build new living cells. Some living things decompose faster than others, and our goal is to use organic material that will decompose easily and quickly.

Avoid thick branches or waxy leaves because they also take a longer time to complete their transition into soil. Soybean and corn stalks are high in lignin and therefore take too long to break down. It is important to stay away from incorporating meat, bones, or dairy products into the bales, since they tend to attract varmints. Avoid the feces of any animal that eats meat, because carnivores carry many more diseases than herbivores that can spread through their feces. Make sure any homemade bales are tightly compressed; this is key because it helps speed decomposition. Tight bales also tend to hold moisture better, but some mechanically bound bales are compressed too tightly. If a finger cannot be wiggled down into the bale, it is likely too tight. Cut the strings and retie them a bit more loosely around the expanded bale.

## MAKING YOUR OWN BALES

Whether you live in Brooklyn, Dublin, Abu Dhabi, or the deserts of Arizona, there are some places where straw bales can be hard to find. No worries. If you have access to organic matter—practically any organic matter—you can form and compress it into planting bales. In my visits to Cambodia and the Philippines, I have seen the locals adopt ingenious techniques for making bales from rice straw. In Costa Rica, they use spent sugar-cane stalks. Basically, if it will rot, you can plant in it. The key is compression. The tightness of the bale causes heat buildup and accelerates the decomposition.

Or you can add compost. The great thing about making your own bales with some compost is that the bales are already partly conditioned. If you press the mixture of compost and fresh organic material into a bale form that holds its shape and supports the plants, the results will be extraordinary. In many instances, the results are even superior to starting with fresh straw bales and fertilizer.

There are many ways to compress a bale. At right you can see a picture of a device I came up with to do it. You can build something like this, or, if you have big feet, you can probably get by with stomping the organic material into a tight mass. Be creative. Make some bales and plant them.

*Above:* This bale-compressing "machine" I devised is pretty simple. Anchor some levers to a tree or post and use them to press organic material into a plastic bin. Tie it up tightly and wrap the whole thing with chicken wire, then plant.

*Left:* A homemade bale will last at least 1 year, and my experiments have proven that this combination of organic material with a little compost can actually outperform conditioned straw bales.

## A Word about Mushrooms

Mushrooms are the fruiting body of the fungi that grow naturally inside many bales of straw. Sometimes bales will be covered in mushrooms a few weeks after the conditioning process begins, while at other times, no mushrooms seem to sprout at all. If the bales sprout mushrooms, this is a very good sign they are ready to plant. If the mushrooms are too thick and pushing up seedlings or spreading spores on the leaves of other plants, you can remove the caps by picking them. Picking the mushroom caps is like trying to kill an apple tree by picking the apples. This will not destroy the mycelium inside the bale, but it may keep the caps from spreading even more spores. Most of the mushrooms that grow naturally on the bales are not edible, but it is possible to grow edible mushrooms on straw bales intentionally.

## Watering: Why More Is Not Better

The biggest mistake made by most new Straw Bale Gardeners is overwatering bales. Once a bale is fully saturated, it will hold between 20 and 45 pounds of water (3 to 5 gallons). The bales lose a bit of water if plant roots are absorbing some of the water. If the weather gets hot, some of the water will evaporate out each day. Once the water is replaced, any excess water added runs directly out the bottom, which carries out soluble nutrients as well as some of the tiny new soil particles and bacteria that are supposed to stay inside the bales. The symptom of this nutrient loss and soil-particle erosion is yellowing and wilting leaves. Because the leaves look similar to plants that are dry and wilting, the instinct is to water heavily for a longer time, which causes more nutrient loss and more soil particles washing out of the bale, exacerbating the problem. The solution is the 1-gallon rule: never apply more than 1 gallon of water per bale per application. Increase the frequency of applications if needed once the plants grow or when the heat of summer arrives, but never increase the dose per application. Always calculate for 1 gallon per bale, and this will prevent excess erosion and nutrient loss. I encourage people to check their bale gardens for moisture levels with a finger poke. Only add water when the bales

When fungus appears on your straw bales midway through the conditioning process, you will know the process is working. Don't worry—the mushrooms go away, and they are harmless.

feel dry. This may be once a week in the spring and fall and every day during the hot summer when tomatoes and cucumbers are using tons of water to make fruit. Increase the frequency, but never increase the dose. Use only 1 gallon per bale per application, and never more.

To make watering easier, use a soaker hose or, even better, a drip irrigation system with an automated timer that you can set if you need to go out of town for an extended time. Run the hose or dripper down the center of the row of bales. The water will get distributed across the width of the bale. Use a new soaker hose each year, because they are easily broken down by intense ultraviolet sunlight. (If you don't replace the hose, one day during its second year of use, it will spring a leak and you'll have a geyser in your garden.) Switch to a dripper-style system; it might cost a bit more to get set up, but it works very well, allowing a drip emitter of any selected flow rate to be placed right on the root of a specific plant. I've had the same drip system in place for 6 years, and it still works just like the day I installed it.

A soaker hose with an automatic timer at the spigot—or any other automated watering system, such as drip irrigation—will make your Straw Bale Garden virtually maintenance free. But if you only have a few bales, hand-watering with sun-warmed water or even watering with a hose and wand takes practically no time at all.

## Fertilizing after Planting

If overwatering occurs, adding additional fertilizer will likely be necessary. If little or no overwatering happens, the nutrient levels inside the conditioned bales should be sufficient without any additional fertilizer. The plants will tell you if they are nutrient deficient. Listen to them by watching and observing their leaves closely. Yellowing on upper leaves and old growth likely means your plants are nitrogen deficient; nitrogen is very soluble and easily washes out. It is easy to identify other nutrient shortages as well, so keep a close eye on the leaves of your garden vegetables. A preemptive plan to add a small amount of a granular balanced fertilizer every 2 or 3 weeks to each bale isn't a terrible idea. It may not be required, but it will certainly head off any potential nutrient issues before they can have any effect on the garden vegetables. If a serious nutrient deficiency pops up, I suggest using a soluble fertilizer that can act quickly to correct the problem.

## Straw Bales: A Weed-Free Environment

There are no weeds to speak of in a Straw Bale Garden, except between the rows of bales. Use something to cover up this area, and try to leave a minimum of 4 feet between rows—5 to 6 feet is even better. (It is rather common for inexperienced Straw Bale Gardeners to plant rows too close together or put too many plants or seeds in any single bale.) Mow the grass or weed growth that pops up between rows of bales. Use old carpeting, cardboard boxes, wood chips, thick layers of loose straw, or anything else that will allow water to permeate but won't allow weeds to get sunlight to cover the mowed spots. Don't use plastic sheeting: it holds moisture, increasing humidity; stinks when the water gets stagnant; and provides a breeding ground for mosquitos. It can also get slippery and become a trip hazard. If you prep the garden properly, there will be virtually zero weeding in a Straw Bale Garden. If your bales sprout oats or wheat, it is because they had leftover seeds in them, so just pluck these out or cut them off and make a wheatgrass smoothie for lunch. The sprouts will normally dry up by midseason anyway. Another option is to use a weed whip if the bales are not yet planted. I just ignore the sprouts, and they eventually go away. These "chia pet" bales with sprouts can also be sprayed or wiped with a homemade herbicide: mix up 1 quart of grocery-store vinegar with 2 tablespoons dish soap and 1 tablespoon table salt. It acts like an herbicide on a hot day and will knock those sprouts out quickly, but it doesn't have any residual effects on the bales, gardeners, or pets, except that it might make you feel like eating a salad for dinner because it smells a bit like salad dressing.

## Upleveling Bales: Adding a Trellis

Cattle panel arches seem to be the newest way many of our biggest gardeners are allowing vining crops to climb above the bales and create an interesting 7-foot-tall archway or tunnel between two rows of bales. Tomatoes, squash, cucumbers, gourds, pumpkins, sweet potatoes, and other crops can benefit when their foliage is kept up off the ground; the plant receives better air circulation, thereby reducing fungal disease and insect issues. In addition, it looks rather nifty and makes harvesting a breeze.

Using standard 8- or 9-foot-tall steel fence posts at both ends of each row of bales also works well. Use 14- or 16-gauge wire between all posts every 8 inches, starting 8 to 10 inches above the bales, all the way to the top. The wire ladder trellis above the bales is great for climbing peas, beans, tomatoes, and other vine crops. Fixing a 2×4 wood board between the posts ensures that when wires are pulled tight between the posts, they won't bend or lean toward the middle. A loose or flimsy trellis could never support the weight of a huge crop of tomatoes or squash nor the wind load from a strong breeze on a 7-foot-tall wall of leaves. There are many more details on setting up a Straw Bale Garden in my previous book, *Straw Bale Gardens Complete*.

A trellis system is not required, but if you rig something up, your Straw Bale Garden will be happier and more neatly contained. I like to run trellis wires between posts at the end of each row. The posts support the wires and help pin the bales together so they keep their shape as long as possible. As you can see below, you can rig something almost as easily on a driveway as you can in your backyard.

# CHAPTER 3

# SOLUTIONS FROM REAL STRAW BALE GARDENERS

OVER THE 10 OR SO YEARS I've been giving presentations and seminars about the Straw Bale Gardens technique, I've spoken to tens of thousands of interested gardeners, and I still love to see people's eyes light up when they first wrap their minds around the concept. Nowadays I often speak to crowds with many already-converted Straw Bale Gardeners, and when I ask for a show of hands from those already growing in bales, they can hardly hold back their excitement and willingness to testify. Almost like clockwork, when I come offstage, a few people with phones or iPads come up to show pictures of their gardens and share stories. Sometimes they even bring their scrapbooks or they show me the newspaper clippings of their garden from the local paper. The stories are amazing, inspiring, and motivating, and they are as varied as the people telling them. One story I recall was from the mother of a young wounded veteran, who was using a wheelchair, who has taken up Straw Bale Gardening and is teaching others how to do it. Then there was the 96-year-old great-great-grandmother I met in Wisconsin. She was in her third year of growing tomatoes in bales. She had already recruited her two daughters, both in their late 70s, to use the Straw Bale Gardens method.

Many of these folks had overcome challenges that so many other gardeners face, challenges that had prevented them from growing traditional gardens in soil until they learned about Straw Bale Gardening. This chapter includes examples that I think represent some of those most common gardening difficulties that many others can relate to. You will probably find that you have something in common with one or more of these folks. Learn how they used Straw Bale Gardening as a solution to their gardening challenges.

Across the world, enterprising Straw Bale Gardeners are finding clever ways to adapt their own gardens to their individual situations. Sometimes the solutions are highly practical, other times they are subtle refinements that give a personal touch to a garden. The addition of colorful red tomato cages in this Straw Bale Garden in Oregon visually transform the garden in a unique and beautiful way. See pages 82 to 85.

# CONQUERING SLOPES IN SWITZERLAND

| | |
|---|---|
| **NAME** | |
| Uschi Sura | |
| **LOCATION** | |
| Glarus, Switzerland | |
| **NUMBER OF BALES** | |
| 15 | |
| **CROPS** | |
| Celeriac, chard, kale, melon, nasturtium, squash | |
| **SBG START DATE** | |
| 2013 | |
| **CHALLENGE** | |
| Steep slope, alpine climate | |
| **WEBSITE** | |
| www.strohballengarten.ch | |

ONLY A MATHEMATICIAN would love the slope problems resulting from a move to Switzerland. Couple the severe slope with a bad back, and Uschi's hopes of having a garden were fading fast. Uschi mitigated the severe slope by using straw bales to level out and elevate her entire growing surface.

A few years ago, Uschi was reading a German magazine featuring an article about "Strohballengärten." Intrigued by the post, which featured the original *Straw Bale Gardens* book, Uschi ordered a copy for herself. When the book arrived, Uschi "devoured it almost in one day." She was fascinated by the idea of growing in bales and was excited to see if it would make gardening on the mountain easier. "At last I had an alternative to the traditional garden," she recalls.

Uschi Sura was born into a gardening family in Germany. Her parents emigrated from Silesia, Poland, and within a few years built a house and started a large garden. Raised by parents who were both passionate gardeners, Uschi and her siblings regularly helped out in the family garden. In fact, the Sura children were encouraged to eat whatever vegetables or fruits they wanted right from the garden while they tended it. Looking back, Uschi says her family was puzzled by the phrase "healthy food"—because everything they ate was already healthy food. They just called it food. With a background like this, it's no surprise that Uschi has become a very capable gardener.

Living for years in rental properties, Uschi had few opportunities to garden. For many years, filling flower pots and loading them into an elevator to the roof of her flat was about the extent of her gardening efforts. Then, around 2013, Uschi and her partner moved to the mountains of Switzerland, a challenging setting with steep terrain and thick clay soil. Anticipating the difficulties of planting and maintaining a mountaintop garden, they both were convinced their garden dreams would remain on hold. "Because of the extreme conditions—clay soil and the severe slope on our property—there really wasn't a possibility to create a traditional garden. My garden was limited to a berry and shrubbery garden," Uschi recalls.

In anticipation of beginning a Straw Bale Garden, Uschi shared her plans with a neighbor, who offered her access to a small part of a meadow for her bales. For her first attempt, Uschi began with five bales. "Due to the volatile weather in the mountains, I had to wait to begin until early May," she says. "I was totally euphoric about starting to Straw Bale Garden, but part of me was skeptical." She confronted many questions: Would this work? Did I use the correct fertilizer? Did I use enough fertilizer? Does any of this make sense? But after a few days, the telltale mushrooms began to emerge, and a few seedheads that had survived in the bales sprouted. As her garden grew, she says, her doubts gradually disappeared.

*Above:* Uschi's pitchfork full of end-of-season straw shows how well decomposed and root friendly the straw becomes.

*Opposite:* The Swiss Alps may be a beautiful location for skiing, but vegetable gardening is a real challenge. A Straw Bale Garden solved the challenge for this enthusiastic grower.

## Joel Says

If you have a friend who thinks *they* have a difficult location for planting a garden, please encourage them read Uschi's story. Uschi lives on top of a mountain, has clay soil and a severe slope, and must carry her water by hand, so tell your friend to stop complaining and get busy gardening.

## Joel Says

Needless to say, I was surprised when Uschi told me that her Straw Bale Garden doesn't really save her much time. I wondered how this could be. The reason? Uschi says it best: "My Straw Bale Garden brings me closer to nature. It gives balance to everyday life. It brings me joy, and I have fun out there. I feel good out there. I feel healthy—I can eat fresh vegetables, fruits, and herbs from my own garden every day, just like I did in my childhood garden growing up! So I spend lots of time among my bales because it makes me happy."

Convinced that growing vegetables in straw would never work, many neighbors, especially the local miners from the area, laughed at her plans. Before long, even the greatest skeptics were convinced. Since then, countless people have been inspired by her mountaintop garden. The neighbors have grown accustomed to her successful garden, and they love to ask questions and talk about it.

Today, Uschi has four separate Straw Bale Gardens across the meadow on the mountain.

### NOTES

At the beginning of the year, there is always a little extra work for Uschi to get the bales conditioned. Uschi uses organic fertilizers, which do a great job preparing the bales during the conditioning process. Without easy access to water, her biggest chore applying water to the bales every day for 10 days. Once the conditioning process is complete, the bales are planted. After that, the effort to maintain the bales is minimal. As you can imagine, Uschi especially appreciates the ability of the bales to hold in moisture. Still, rainy seasons are welcome because they mean that Uschi seldom needs to carry water to her bales—an extra advantage when growing a Straw Bale Garden in a remote location.

Uschi stays away from all pesticides and uses a moon calendar to help determine the best planting times.

### CROPS

Amazed every year by her garden, Uschi is especially proud of the extraordinary size and yield of her plants. Uschi tries new crops each year, and she has discovered that some grow wonderfully in her Straw Bale Garden. "This year I planted for the first time Inka–Gurke

*Right:* Uschi no longer needs to drive down a mountain to get fresh salad greens at the market: now she grows her own.

*Opposite, top:* The slope of the mountain makes any exposed soil wash away quickly, but the bales hold their position with just a little staking.

The Litchi tomato (*Solanum sisymbriifolium*).

Inka-Gurke (*Cyclanthera pedata*) is a fruit-bearing vine similar to a cucumber.

## A VEGAN SBG?

Innovative ideas excite Uschi—that's why the novelty of Straw Bale Gardens first captured her imagination. But after 4 years of Straw Bale Gardening, Uschi felt her confidence growing and wanted to do some experimentation with her bales. After asking many questions about conditioning the bales, she set up a trial experiment. On nine bales, Uschi applied only vegan organic fertilizer—that is, fertilizer derived entirely from vegetable matter with no bonemeal, blood meal, or animal litter. On eight bales, Uschi applied standard organic fertilizer that can contain natural ingredients from animals. On her remaining bales, she continued to use conventional (synthetic) fertilizer. The result?

Uschi was very pleased to discover that "the vegan fertilizer worked wonderfully"—just as well as the other methods.

## Joel Says

Uschi's perspective on healthy food is so important and reminds me of a favorite saying about what we should eat: "Eat food made from plants, not made in plants."

*Opposite, top:* Straw bales are made the same way all around the world. These bales just have a better view than most.

*Opposite, middle:* Combining vegetables that grow well together is a strategy most try to implement. It isn't unusual to put multiple plants in the same bale.

*Opposite, bottom:* In Switzerland, they just call it "chard"!

*Below:* While it is a beautiful storybook setting, a mountaintop garden has many challenges. Slope, soil, water, and climate all contribute difficulties.

(*Cyclanthera pedata*). It is incredible because these plants do not want to stop growing. Two years ago, I grew Litchi tomato, and they taste delicious. It was the same phenomenon; it grew and flourished even more when I cleared the garden at the end of October."

### LIFE ON A MOUNTAIN

Uschi lives in one of the most beautiful places on the planet, as you can plainly see from the pictures that are featured here in her profile and elsewhere in this book. Alone, straw bales are not especially attractive, but even a simple Straw Bale Garden looks stunning with Uschi's incredible mountain vista in the background.

### STROHBALLENGÄRTEN

Uschi was so enthusiastic with the results of her very first Straw Bale Garden that she designed her own website, www.strohballengarten.ch.

The website was originally created to be a place where Uschi could share her Straw Bale Garden experiences. Surprised by the immediate interest in and heavy traffic to her site, Uschi was soon answering questions and posting even more information about her mountaintop Straw Bale Garden. Eventually, Uschi's wonderful online resource captured the attention of the European press, and soon journalists and bloggers were sharing Uschi's story and her incredibly successful Straw Bale Garden. Today, Uschi continues to provide stories about her Straw Bale Garden to magazine editors, newspapers, and other media.

## COLD-CLIMATE GARDENING

| NAME | |
|---|---|
| Beth Hanson Fox | |
| **LOCATION** | |
| Nova Scotia, Canada | |
| **NUMBER OF BALES** | |
| 20 | |
| **CROPS** | |
| Beans, carrots, cucumbers, pumpkins, squash, tomatoes | |
| **SBG START DATE** | |
| 2015 | |
| **CHALLENGE** | |
| Cold northern climate, short growing season | |

COLD NORTHERN CLIMATES make for long winters and short growing seasons. No surprise there. But when they discovered Straw Bale Gardening, one feature stood out and led a couple of Canadian friends to give the method a try. During the conditioning process, the straw bales begin to be colonized by bacteria and the bales naturally heat up (see more in Chapter 2), giving most northern vegetable gardeners a significant head start on the gardening season. Transplanting or seeding into the surface of a bale that is already warm, instead of into soil that is still cold, encourages quicker root production and faster plant development. Getting ahead of the weeds isn't a concern because, of course, there are virtually no weeds in a Straw Bale Garden.

Beth and a friend were hoping to team up and build raised beds a few years back, when her friend showed up one day for their commute to work with a copy of *Straw Bale Gardens Complete*. By the time they got to work that day, they had decided "This just might be worth a try." Betting that it would be cheaper, easier, and faster, they were willing to make the attempt. Since both were working moms, it seemed like a perfect option for them.

Beth Hanson Fox grew up with a mother who gardened extensively. Beth had three siblings, and her mother wanted "as much healthy food as possible for her family." She recalls, "We loathed having to weed the garden as part of our summertime chores list . . . but then we would feast on fresh beans, peas, carrots, and everything else." Beth acknowledges that she didn't fully appreciate the gift her mother gave her until she had kids of her own. Now she's teaching her own children how to garden, with one minor upgrade: no weeds! She has also recruited her mother to the Straw Bale Gardening team, convincing her to try a few bales for her garden this year. Another of Beth's friends in Vancouver, BC, has also become a convert.

At previous homes, Beth used to build raised beds. "The Straw Bale Gardens method takes care of this with no investment," she says. "It is also lovely with the kids. They can help, and they are far less messy than if they were tromping around in the dirt. They love to run to the garden when we get in at the end of the day and check on everything while they steal peas to eat. I think the bales make it very accessible to them, and I don't worry about them stepping on the plants. . . . It just works really well with our family."

The Straw Bale Garden is located in Beth's front yard, so she gets many questions from people about the garden. Dogwalkers ask if they can take a closer look and are surprised by the whole concept. Beth says that she "always invites them to come back and snoop again if they want to see the progress. Many are impressed, and I can see them thinking, 'I wonder if this could work for me.'"

Beth also loves the freedom she has with her Straw Bale Garden. "It is so self-sufficient with the timer and irrigation, I don't have to

## Joel Says

For most of us in the United States, when we think of Canada, we think of "our friends to the north." It's worth noting, however, that 64 percent of all Canadians actually live below the latitude of Seattle, Washington. There are a whole lot of Canadians who have an exceptionally good climate for gardening. As Beth can testify, with the first sliver of sunshine in the spring, the weeds burst out of the ground and establish themselves. There are days in the early spring when the weeds in her garden seem to grow knee high overnight. Most tender vegetable transplants and seeds must wait until the safe planting date arrives and the soil has warmed up before planting. The weeds, the climate, and cold soil are all issues Beth faces every year.

*Opposite:* The heat generated by the decomposing straw in the early season gives gardeners in colder climates, such as Canada, a head start on the season.

Cherry tomatoes are the perfect "treat while you work" crop to grow when you're gardening with children.

think about it," she says. "If we get too much or not enough rain, it is way more adaptable than my raised beds ever were. I've never had much extra time to garden, but now I know I get much better yield and have none of the guilt that I had before watching the weeds take over . . . a huge plus."

### CROPS

Beth grows mainly tomatoes, beans, cucumbers, and squash, but many other things sneak in around those main crops. She is excited about her carrots this year, and a giant pumpkin!

### GETTING A HEAD START

Using the "Straw Bale Greenhouse" technique as described in *Straw Bale Gardens Complete,* gardeners can plant even earlier than normal. The covers protect young seedlings and tender transplants from freezing overnight temperatures. They also hold in the heat generated by the bales, keeping the cold air away. This allows successful planting 10 to 20 days earlier than traditional gardening, depending on the crop.

Beth admits, "I was unsure how the conditioning would actually work since I had bales that had been left out all winter, and they were frozen. It was slow getting them going, but my digital meat thermometer started to show they were heating up, and I knew I had something cooking.

"The first year, the bales with the mini greenhouse of fabric over top let me get an early start. Certainly in the Nova Scotia climate we have a late spring. This year I had a very late start due to a busy life. Compared to my neighbor's traditional in-ground garden, also planted late, my garden has caught up nicely, while hers is still way behind. She commented to my husband recently that our Straw Bale Garden was sure doing well!"

### EATING LOCAL

Beth says, "My daughter likes to stand in the garden and say, 'It doesn't get any more local than this, Mom.'" In many cases, dinner can come from the garden and be served at the dinner table an hour later. Expanding a Straw Bale Garden is easy: just buy a few more bales as needed. Like the example her mother set for Beth and her siblings, Beth wants to provide healthy, local, sustainable food for her family. She says, "I try to buy from local producers whenever I can, but growing our own food has so many benefits. I love showing my children where food comes from, how good it tastes when picked fresh, and the satisfaction of eating what we've worked hard to grow."

## GROWING A GIANT PUMPKIN

Beth has one minor gardening obsession she freely admits to: she has a personal goal to grow a giant pumpkin. She's not after a lot of pumpkins but instead really wants just one *huge* pumpkin. In the past, she's tried raised beds made of tires and other methods, but she has yet to get anything larger than a basketball. She has her hopes up for this year: "I'm keeping an eye on the giant pumpkin I've got started in the bales. It's early, but it tripled in size in just the past week!" The bales make it easy for her to add extra fertilizer, and the trellis helps keep the fruit off the ground and away from slugs. She might need to rig up something hefty to hold up her giant pumpkin if it keeps growing at this pace. I can't wait to hear her results this fall.

*Left, top:* Peas thrive in the bales, and, in under 50 days from seeding, you'll be greeted by the most amazing fresh taste nature provides.

*Left, bottom:* One of the easiest ways to extend the season is with a few jars of cucumbers turned into pickles—simple but delicious treats with a winter barbeque.

*Above:* One should always plant a few sunflowers in every garden, but especially whenever children are involved—kids love sunflowers.

## Joel Says

The intensity of the sun is so much stronger in northern climates in early spring and summer than it is the rest of the year. One week of growing-season extension in the spring is about equal to three weeks of growing season in the late fall. Stop worrying about having green tomatoes hanging on in the fall. Instead, plant a week or two earlier in the spring. Be the first on the block with ripe tomatoes next summer—of course, this makes you the winner!

# FLOOD-ZONE GARDEN

| NAME |
| --- |
| Marjon Cootjans-van Stiphout |
| **LOCATION** |
| Dommelen, Netherlands |
| **NUMBER OF BALES** |
| 60+ |
| **CROPS** |
| Cabbage, cucumbers, green beans, leaf crops, peas, peppers, potatoes, squash (all varieties), strawberries, tomatoes |
| **SBG START DATE** |
| 2013 |
| **CHALLENGE** |
| Garden is prone to flooding |
| **FACEBOOK** |
| Co' Cootjes Moestuin op Strobalen |

SITED ALONG A RIVER in the Netherlands, Marjon's garden was plagued by seasonal flooding, which regularly wiped out crops. She discovered that planting a Straw Bale Garden is a great way to neutralize the devastating impact of an influx of water. With the inherent water-wise efficiencies of straw bales, gardeners can effectively utilize plots in flood-prone areas, making them productive once more, without concern about the garden being ruined.

It was at a rental house in Belgium where Marjon Cootjansvan Stiphout had her first opportunity to plant a vegetable garden about 20 years ago. The house her family had rented there had a large garden, but it was springtime when they realized part of the garden was meant for planting vegetables. She had a little introduction back then, but 5 years ago, she was able to start vegetable gardening in a serious way.

She lives now in Dommelen, a small village in the southern part of the Netherlands, on 3.2 acres of land. A sizeable stream about 20 feet wide runs through her property. The banks of this water source provide a beautiful setting for her dream vegetable garden. Marjon spent lots of time turning up the soil, preparing to plant her first large and beautiful vegetable garden. She discovered too late that when a heavy rain came, her gentle stream turned into a 180-foot-wide flood plain that could persist for a week before receding. This didn't happen every year, but after spending a great amount of effort to plant a large garden, knowing the whole time that a few rainy days could wipe out all her effort made her look for alternatives.

When one of those floods came, Marjon lost all her tomato plants in just 2 days. In search of a solution to her problem, she went to a garden show in Belgium to enjoy a tomato fair. She found a bookseller there, and while browsing the inventory, *Straw Bale Gardens* caught her eye, and she read a few pages. She says now that she "was directly inspired."

This idea of using bales seemed to Marjon to be a perfect solution to her flooding problems. Even so, she had some doubts about whether the Straw Bale Gardens method outlined in the book was actually going to work. She forged ahead and followed the step-by-step instructions in the book. In her experience, she says, "not all of the bales heated up the same, and I was skeptical, because some of the bales never did warm up. I was very excited to see what would happen and what would grow." Her family and friends were all very skeptical too, and they thought the whole idea would not last for one season. Now, after a few years, the exact opposite has happened. Now she claims that "everyone who sees my garden is flabbergasted. Ta-da!"

A Straw Bale Garden has solved every problem she encountered with her traditional garden, particularly because of its ability to

*Above:* While the straw bales will wick floodwater up into the bale to the plant roots, irrigation will again be helpful once the flood recedes.

*Opposite:* Low country land is usually unfarmable, but this SBG in the Netherlands relies on the height of the bales to protect the plants when waters rise.

handle possible floods when her lovely stream goes over its banks. The floods still come, but the plants survive perfectly once the water recedes; all the plants are just fine planted on top of the bales. Marjon also no longer has to weed or bend to the ground to plant. She loves that she can change the look of the garden every spring by simply moving bales around. Without having to worry about crop rotation every spring, she can keep plants that need sun in the same sunny spots and not worry about soilborne disease. She likes that she can use the compost from the bales in other garden areas as mulch.

## CROPS

"Most of what I plant grows to be gigantic, and I only need to put a little extra fertilizer in the water during the growing season. My favorite thing is to see the open-mouth stare that always happens when my friends come to inspect my garden!"

## THE WORKSHOP TOUR

Marjon gives workshops around her country and other parts of Europe on "Happy and Healthy Living," and she gives attendees her whole story and a look at the beautiful gardens she has created. She does cooking demonstrations in the workshop as well, and guess where she gets the ingredients for her healthy recipes? Marjon has spread her love of Straw Bale Gardening to neighbors and friends all over Europe and South America and shows lots of her best photos to all of her friends on her Facebook page, Co' Cootjes Moestuin op Strobalen.

*Top:* Using bales to edge out an existing perennial or annual flower garden is a novel and useful idea.

*Bottom:* A saturated or conditioned bale won't float away, but a fresh straw bale will float . . . for a while.

## FAVORITE SAYINGS

Marjon says, "Gardening gives me freedom and 'me time' to order my thoughts. I like to be in nature within the sounds and the smells. Planting seeds and growing the food that I will eat makes me very happy." Her favorite poem by Alfred Austin says, "The glory of gardening: hands in the dirt, head in the sun, heart with nature. To nurture a garden is to feed not just the body, but the soul."

*Top:* Taking a piece of property back from Mother Nature's unforgiving ways can feel empowering.

*Bottom:* When the water rises, a gardener's hopes usually fall. For a bale gardener it means a few days off from having to water.

## Joel Says

Marjon and I have emailed back and forth a few times over the years. One of her messages came when the flood waters were surrounding all her bales. She was worried, but I knew they would be okay. I tried to lessen her fears, because I knew that as long as the bales were conditioned so they weren't full of air, they wouldn't float away. She is from Holland, a region in the Netherlands, which is truly the horticultural research capital of the world. When it comes to horticulture, as the saying goes, "If you ain't Dutch, you ain't much!" One of my goals with the Straw Bale Gardens method is to get the nod of approval from the Dutch, and I know for sure that I have at least one fan there so far.

# ROCKY MOUNTAINS & ROCKY SOIL

| | |
|---|---|
| **NAME** | |
| Odebt Massey | |
| **LOCATION** | |
| Yoder, Colorado | |
| **NUMBER OF BALES** | |
| 50 | |
| **CROPS** | |
| Cabbage, squash, tomatoes, and several other crops | |
| **SBG START DATE** | |
| 2013 | |
| **CHALLENGE** | |
| Rock-hard Rocky Mountain soil | |
| **FACEBOOK** | |
| Eastern Colorado Straw Bale Gardening | |

Combined with the extremes in climate from being at 6,000 feet above sea level, Colorado gardening can be pretty precarious. "I've taken every course on gardening and learn mostly by trial and error," Odebt Massey says, but "I'm just a normal backyard gardener."

ONE OF THE MOST ALLURING (and frustrating) aspects of gardening is that you can never really predict what is going to work. Plants that should thrive sometimes fail. Others you never contemplate growing will volunteer in your garden out of the blue and settle in perfectly. The only way to know for certain what works is simply to try it. Odebt Massey installed many trial gardens over the years and had a lot of errors. But her trial Straw Bale Garden was, as she says, "By far the most successful and productive method of gardening for me ever!"

One day, Odebt was at Lowe's (one of the big US home improvement stores), where she loves to leaf through the books and find inspiration. My book *Straw Bale Gardens Complete* almost jumped out at her, so she picked it up. "I decided to buy it and immediately read it from cover to cover. I have worn that book out," she says.

Although Odebt helped out in the garden as a child in California, it wasn't until she was married and moved to her first home that she planted her first vegetable garden on her own. Odebt is a woman of many talents, gardening being only one. A former American Kernel Club professional dog handler, a miniature replica–house builder, and a fairy-garden expert, Odebt lives in a beautiful spot in the foothills of the Rocky Mountains. Odebt has a big family and calls Yoder, Colorado, home. Yoder is a small unincorporated community of around 1,000 people at an altitude of just over 6,000 feet.

With sufficient space to garden, Odebt was looking forward to installing a big garden until she discovered that the soil in her area is a disaster. She tried amending it for years to no avail. "I tried and tried to condition our soil here on the eastern high plains, but each

### Joel Says

Odebt's first garden was at a rental house. Renting a property means that a gardener is usually working within parameters set by the landlord. This was certainly the case for Odebt, who found she would have to table most of her ideas and keep the garden pretty small. The saying "Gardeners dream bigger dreams than emperors" rings especially true for any gardener renting space.

## Joel Says

One thing that Odebt didn't mention specifically but likely was very helpful in her climate is the fact that the bales heat up as they begin to decompose. The warmth continues for 5 to 6 weeks after the conditioning process has begun, so her seeds and seedlings were growing in the bales with a bit of heat helping to encourage their root growth for the first several weeks of growth. In a climate at elevation where the temperatures can be very warm during the day but still very cold at night, this is likely a very important factor that has led to successful growing in Odebt's Straw Bale Garden.

year it seemed all the work I had done the prior year had all leached away." Rock-hard soil was a big problem for Odebt, and as she says, "I'm getting too old to dig in hard ground." In addition, Odebt has a touch of arthritis, so doing the physical work a garden requires is really out of the question. Getting down on her hands and knees in the garden wasn't something she looked forward to at all.

Luckily for Odebt, "the bales solved this problem, and many other problems." The climate in Yoder is harsh, with very low humidity and drying winds that suck the moisture right out of the soil.

*Right, top:* Odebt doesn't do things small, starting with a 50-bale garden. She has more gumption than most!

*Right, bottom:* Ground cloth covering the aisles between rows of bales makes weeding obsolete.

The bales hold enough water to keep the roots moist while still draining well. The inherent superior drainage of the bales offsets any accidental overwatering or heavy rainfall that used to flood her traditional flat-earth gardens.

### THE 50-BALE SOLUTION

Odebt says she didn't doubt that the Straw Bale Gardens method was going to work, but she did question whether or not she was in over her head when she saw those first 50 bales getting delivered. There was a little peer pressure as well. "Everyone I knew was interested in what I was doing. They wanted to know all the details—especially my results," Odebt recalls. "Others said they had heard about it and wanted to try it. Needless to say, my results convinced them that, indeed, it was a great method."

After the initial setup and conditioning, Odebt spends very little time tending the garden. The long hours she spent working a traditional flat-earth garden can never be reclaimed. "Now, I spend a lot more time simply enjoying the garden," she says.

In terms of cost, buying all the bales and getting them delivered was a bit of an investment. However, once she calculates all the time she saves not weeding and not battling crop loss due to poor soil and factors in all the other benefits of using the bales, it isn't even close. Odebt says, "All in all, I think there is no extra cost of using the Straw Bale Gardens method."

### CROPS

Odebt's only wish is that she could have a bit of a longer growing season, but she isn't willing to give up her gorgeous view of the Rockies for a little more garden time. Satisfied with her great production of squash, tomatoes, cabbage, and several other crops, Odebt has no plans to ever go back to growing in the soil.

"Every single year, I am amazed! I have used the Straw Bale Gardens method for four seasons, and each season I am amazed at the ease, the happiness of the plants, and the bounty I get in return," says Odebt. I think she's convinced!

*Top:* You better *bee*lieve adding flowers to a vegetable garden is a good idea. Attracting pollinators can improve yields.

*Bottom:* An insider's view under the tented cover of a Straw Bale Greenhouse. Get more details on this technique in my other books.

### FACEBOOK GROUP

Odebt set up her own Facebook group, Eastern Colorado Straw Bale Gardening, to share her success and inspire others in her area to take over the whole state of Colorado with the Straw Bale Gardens method.

# SEARCHING FOR GOLD IN STRAW BALES

| NAME | |
|---|---|
| Sandy Golay | |
| **LOCATION** | |
| Pittsburg, Kansas | |
| **NUMBER OF BALES** | |
| 100+ | |
| **CROPS** | |
| Acorn squash, Asian long beans, basil, bell peppers, butternut squash, canary melons, cucumbers, garlic, potatoes, spaghetti squash, summer squash, sweet candy onions, sweet onions, tomatoes, zucchini | |
| **SBG START DATE** | |
| 2011 | |
| **CHALLENGE** | |
| Efficient farming | |
| **FACEBOOK** | |
| Golay Gardens | |

GARDENING FOR PROFIT on a challenging hillside is a big job. When heavy spring rains kept rolling through May, Sandy Golay's two 60-foot-long garden rows eroded away. That erosion would have serious economic consequences for Sandy's Golay Gardens, and fixing it would take away valuable spring planting time. It so happens that at the same time, Sandy discovered the Straw Bale Gardens method.

Even though she grew up in garden-happy Kansas, Sandy did little gardening until she reached adulthood. At 19 years of age, she found herself pregnant with a son, economically challenged, and living in a mobile home on an old farmstead some distance from the nearest town. With a slim budget for groceries, she made a decision to spend some of her food dollars on a few packs of vegetable seeds and some onion sets. Thankfully, the soil next to the old barn on that farmstead was rich and fertile, and her garden provided an abundance of produce. Over the course of the summer, Sandy realized that she has a knack for gardening, and I'm certain that beautiful soil she found was a significant factor.

Over the years, Sandy gardened in many places around Kansas. Some of her gardens weren't so wonderful because the soil was not productive. Most of these soils were hard clay, compacted, and less than ideal for a vegetable garden. Without the addition of lots of compost and long hours of preparation work, these gardens were downright inhospitable to plants. But neither Sandy nor her family ever went hungry, because she knew how to make even the worst soil provide for her family.

Admittedly, Sandy and her late husband, Bob, were a bit skeptical and impatient the first season they tried Straw Bale Gardening. With the torrential spring rains and eroding slope, they were desperate for the new method to work.

They hauled in 90 bales that first year, laid them out right in the area that had eroded, and nervously followed the instructions provided in my first book. When Sandy thought the conditioning process wasn't doing anything, she pushed her hand down inside the bale and felt the reassuring heat. With conditioning well underway, she knew they were doing it correctly.

A few of her friends openly doubted the whole process, wondering how Sandy could even try to grow vegetables without soil. But no soil also means no soilborne diseases. Thus, there's no need to rotate crops. So for folks gardening with limited space, Straw Bale Gardening truly is an ideal solution.

"We were able to grow an amazing surplus of veggies that year, and then we used the same bales in the same spot for potatoes the following year, with another wonderful harvest," Sandy recalls.

The beautiful compost that remains when the bales are completely decomposed is a terrific addition to build up the soil in any

*Above:* Over the years, Sandy's traditional garden soils have benefited from the bountiful compost left behind by her bale gardens.

*Opposite:* Cabbage likes bales! Sandy quickly discovered that some crops were much better in bales than in the heavy Kansas soils.

## Joel Says

One of my all-time favorite Straw Bale Gardeners is Sandy Golay. She was one of the earliest adopters and has become a big supporter over the years. Today she runs Golay Gardens, which sells produce at the Pittsburg, Kansas, farmers market almost every weekend. She is truly a professional gardener at this point, but as she pointed out to me, this wasn't always the case. I know that she is a fan of my Straw Bale Gardens method, but I also consider her a friend at this point. I might just show up at the farmer's market in Pittsburg one day to surprise her!

garden. After this first experience, Sandy was sold on the concept of Straw Bale Gardening. Sandy's been pitching the concept to other gardeners who struggle with soil issues ever since.

### CROPS

Crops that fared poorly in the native clay soil thrived in the bales. "Harvesting potatoes was so easy, and they came out sparkling clean," Sandy says, smiling.

### THE FARMERS MARKET

As a vendor at the farmers market, Sandy can share her gardening ideas with a large audience every week. Once, Sandy and Bob hosted their local garden club so members could tour their Straw Bale Garden to see how well it produced. Several of the gardeners who were on that tour have now become fans of the method and are using it in their own gardens.

### GOLAY GARDENS

Sandy's husband, Bob, passed away not long ago, but she continues with Golay Gardens. People look forward to seeing her and her signature harvest items at the market most Saturdays. Sandy makes her own line of products, including her Sweet Heat Jam, Premium Mixed Jam, Sandy's Super Naturals Body Butters and Sugar Scrubs, SpritzIt Body Spray, and Linen Spray.

Sandy says, "Being outside in nature is very important to me, and the garden work also keeps me in great healthy shape."

## SOURCING BALES

Sandy found a farmer who was willing to make her and Bob a deal on bales if they only took the bottom layer of his straw-bale piles. Why? The bottom bales had gotten wet and had a few rocks stuck to them, so they couldn't be sold to stores for bedding material.

*Top:* Other than a few sprouts from wheat seeds that might have remained in the bales, there really aren't any weeds to pull, so time spent tending the bales is minimal.

*Bottom:* One thing Sandy says amazed her the most was how little watering it took to maintain the level of moisture needed by plants in the bales.

# BATTLING THE LONE STAR SUN

| | |
|---|---|
| **NAME** | |
| Margaret | |
| **LOCATION** | |
| Celeste, Texas | |
| **NUMBER OF BALES** | |
| 50 | |
| **CROPS** | |
| Beans, peppers, potatoes, squash, tomatoes, and more | |
| **SBG START DATE** | |
| 2016 | |
| **CHALLENGE** | |
| Extreme Texas heat, fire ants | |

SWELTERING TEXAS SUMMER HEAT in July and August caused Margaret's crops to wilt by midday. Shade helps, but planting a garden near trees for afternoon shade isn't a great solution either; inevitably, understory planting pits trees against plants. Digging damages tree roots, and plants compete for moisture with thirsty, well-established trees. Finally, heavy midsummer rains often ruin fruit because growing in contact with wet soil causes rot and rolls out the welcome mat for pests and disease.

Straw Bale Gardens can be sited anywhere, and they neutralize even Texas-size environmental stressors. In anticipation of the relentless heat during July and August, positioning bales near large trees and in areas where shade is reliable gives crops much-needed relief from midday sun. Happily, trees and straw bales get along just fine: bales do no harm to tree roots, and tree roots have no effect on the crops up in the bales.

Everything is bigger in Texas, including the thermometers and rain gauges. For Margaret and others who garden in northeast Texas, the combination of heavy black-clay soil and Texas-size thunderstorms makes traditional gardening problematic because there are so many environmental stressors for crops. Furthermore, finding the exact right spot to site a garden in Texas is a tricky endeavor: choosing poorly can result in a burned-up garden by midsummer.

Years ago, Margaret was a young single mother of two on a limited budget. Out of necessity, she started gardening and realized the garden could provide not only an abundance of food but also an important education for her two young children. Unfortunately, on many occasions, Margaret's garden was flooded out. "There were times when I couldn't even get to the garden without getting stuck in the mud. Then the weeds would take over," she says.

A trip to northern Wisconsin to visit her son and his family would forever change the way Margaret gardened. Shopping at a local farm store, Margaret came across the book *Straw Bale Gardens Complete*. Not surprisingly, her chronic severe back pain and arthritis provided extra motivation for her to leave the store with that book.

As Margaret read about the many advantages to the Straw Bale Gardens method, she said, "We had to have it." When spring rolled around, she got even more excited to give it a try, realizing, "I can use my seated cart and simply roll my way up and down the rows when planting and harvesting." Great idea, Margaret!

### SHARING THE SBG EXPERIENCE

With one year under her belt, Margaret is enjoying excellent results in her second year of growing with her Straw Bale Garden. "Everything I have planted has had the best results I've ever experienced," she says.

*Opposite:* The intense Texas heat can melt any vegetable gardener's hopes, but planting around trees for shade has its own set of problems. Unless you are planting in straw bales, that is.

## A TEXAS STRAW BALE GARDEN

The chief concern Margaret had before Straw Bale Gardening was whether the bales would withstand the extreme Texas heat. It wasn't long before Margaret realized the simple straw bales were fully capable of handling Texas growing conditions. As promised, the bales have proven to hold water very well, while several large trees on Margaret's property provide the garden with late-afternoon shade—key in the Texas summer heat.

Thrilled with the results, Margaret said, "In our very first year of trying Straw Bale Gardening, it amazed us. We had the best harvest we had ever had! To us, nothing beats the flavor of homegrown produce. The fact that we could enjoy all that produce without all the backbreaking work . . . we were hooked! We will never do a traditional garden again. Why is that? Weeds were always a problem to keep up with in a traditional garden, but with a Straw Bale Garden, we have no weeds at all. I just mow the grass in between the rows."

Margaret is not shy about sharing her success, and although a few neighbors have been skeptical, there's no denying the advantages of growing in bales. "With all the rain, my neighbors had trouble getting into their gardens this year—but not me. And while some of their crops were rotting on the wet ground, mine were perfectly fine, high and dry on the bales."

Naturally, Margaret has shared her success with friends on Facebook, where she explains that once the garden is set up and planted, it doesn't take much time at all to maintain her garden. Margaret recognizes the personal benefits of gardening, saying, "To me, Straw Bale Gardening is very relaxing and motivating. To know that this is something I accomplished after taking a chance on Straw Bale Gardening—that's very rewarding. I also enjoy sharing the produce with family and friends."

### CROPS

Everything Margaret has grown has done well. She has 50 bales of assorted vegetables, but her tomatoes, squash, cucumbers, peppers, potatoes, and green beans are all going gangbusters. I would suggest some okra and collard greens, because I know lots of folks in the South love those favorites, and I hear they both grow well in the bales. By the looks of her pictures, she has some Texas-size vegetable plants already flourishing.

## STRAW BALES VERSUS MOISTURE

Once they are well conditioned, straw bales will hold moisture exceptionally well, protecting even the thirstiest crops from the dry heat of summer. Because of the raised height of the bales, excess rainwater will drain quickly, and those early-spring rains, no matter how heavy, will have no detrimental effects on the bale or the crops. In fact, Margaret was able to plant her Straw Bale Garden while her neighbors anxiously waited for their muddy gardens to dry out. The raised height and the trellising above the bales keep the harvest high and dry, eliminating the potential for rot while discouraging pests and disease.

## FIRE ANTS

There are certain environmental concerns that have to be addressed no matter how you choose to garden. Invading fire ants are problematic for traditional gardens as well as Straw Bale Gardens in certain areas. Ask anyone who has gotten stung by fire ants and they'll tell you that the sting can hurt for weeks. In addition, fire ants can damage crops such as okra, potatoes, and eggplant. In Margaret's case, she found that treating areas of concern immediately for ants has mitigated any problems.

Ants are normally not a problem, as they are helpful in decomposing things, after all—but fire ants can be dangerous.

# WHEN A TRADITIONAL GARDEN IS OUT OF REACH

| NAME |
|------|
| William Fleming |
| **LOCATION** |
| Mountain Home, Arkansas |
| **NUMBER OF BALES** |
| 45 |
| **CROPS** |
| Bush tomatoes, cucumbers, okra, peppers, potatoes, squash, sweet potatoes, yard-long beans |
| **SBG START DATE** |
| 2014 |
| **CHALLENGE** |
| Poor soil, flooding rains |
| **FACEBOOK** |
| Straw Bale Miracle Garden |

AFTER YEARS OF BATTLING poor soil conditions and flooding rains, William had given up gardening. But instead of quitting gardening, William quit working in adverse conditions. After reading about Straw Bale Gardens in 2014, William was hopeful the method would allow him to come out of gardening retirement. "I read all about this new way to garden using bales and thought, 'This sounds too good to be true.' I thought it was crazy to try growing in straw bales, but I was willing to try it. Great balls of fire—it worked! I started back into gardening again from that day on."

William and his wife enjoy living on a giant rock—some call it Arkansas. Gardening in William's neck of the woods is, unquestionably, a challenge. Almost anywhere in the state, if you dig down even a little ways, you will hit solid rock. Talk about tough growing conditions.

Back in the early 1990s, William decided to give vegetable gardening a try. He used his existing soil and tilled it up to make a garden every year. Given the amount of rock, flat-earth gardening in the Southern Ozark Mountains was always a lot of hard work for William. Additionally, the rocky, nonproductive soil made it difficult to grow edibles with the kind of success William had always envisioned. Three successive years of flooding rains saturated the garden and wiped out his crops. Frustrated and discouraged, William hung up his hoe and quit gardening completely in 2010.

Four years later, eager to try his newfound gardening system, William threw himself into setting up a Straw Bale Garden. In the beginning, he says, everybody thought he was crazy, and he even had a few doubts himself. Worried the bales wouldn't work, he overplanted "just to make sure something would grow." His garden turned into a jungle, and he had "gangbuster production," as he calls it.

William and his wife now plant a 45-bale garden every spring. It takes him 60 to 90 minutes a day to complete the conditioning process in the spring. After the bales are planted, William spends just a few minutes each day tending the garden.

William has had a few health problems over the past couple of years, and working a traditional garden—particularly one with the rocky, laborious conditions of an Arkansas garden—is not something most doctors would recommend. With a Straw Bale Garden, William says, "It isn't work; it's relaxation."

William has also done some experimenting of his own, and he highly recommends building simple wood boxes from recycled pallets. The boxes hold second- and third-year bales and can be used over and over this way without the chance of the bales collapsing. His idea is a good one, and many people have followed his advice on this with great results.

*Opposite:* These cattle-panel archways between SBG rows are perfect for training vines and also help keep the space around the gardens clear for easy accessibility.

## Joel Says

I've received dozens of letters from older, seasoned gardeners who share their stories about how they have come out of gardening retirement thanks to their new Straw Bale Garden because it is much less work.

# Joel Says

Overplanting is a common tendency for new Straw Bale Gardeners. Don't feel bad if you overplant. In time, you'll learn to trust the method and scale back on the number of plants. Learning to gauge plant size at maturity is a skill. Over time, you'll plant to accommodate the eventual size of each plant when mature.

## CROPS

William particularly likes his tomatoes (bush type), yard-long green beans, squash, zucchini, cucumbers, okra, potatoes, sweet potatoes, and peppers of all types. He likes to share his produce with his friends and neighbors.

## STRAW BALE MIRACLE GARDEN FACEBOOK GROUP

As all the worst parts about gardening went away, all the best parts about gardening remained for William. He was finally able to enjoy the successful edible harvest he had envisioned. In fact, William considered his return to gardening—successful gardening—to be somewhat of a miracle. Not surprisingly, William wanted to share his renewed excitement for gardening with his friends. In turn, their excitement over seeing William's garden success led William to begin a Facebook group for Straw Bale Gardeners called "Straw Bale Miracle Garden."

Today, William is the administrator for the group, which includes more than 10,000 of his closest online friends. Overseeing a group that large is not easy, so to keep up with all the questions people ask, he brought on some other experienced Straw Bale Gardeners to help. Together, they have grown the group into one of the largest groups on social media devoted to the Straw Bale Gardens technique.

As the founder of the group, William loves to help others experience their own garden miracles with the easy success found with Straw Bale Gardens.

*Above:* Determinate tomatoes do not vine in the way that indeterminates do, so they can produce a lot of fruit in a small footprint. Bush plants, like these Romas, ripen at the same time, more or less, which makes them perfect for cooking up a big batch of sauce or salsa.

*Right:* William has used wire cattle panels to create an arch from one row of bales to another. These create wonderful trellises for tomatoes, cucumbers, or squash.

Recycled wood pallets, cut in half and joined end to end, then supported with posts or stakes, make excellent "planter boxes" to hold second-, third-, and even fourth-year bales. Potatoes do exceptionally well in the well-decomposed straw from previous gardens. Regular or sweet potatoes are equally happy.

## Joel Says

Indeterminate hybrid tomato plants are *huge*, so planting more than one per bale, or even planting them on adjoining bales, can be too crowded. Smaller heirloom varieties or determinate growers are much smaller, and you might easily squeeze two into one bale. Remember, if you are going to plant extra things or interplant your main crops, use seeds, as they are inexpensive. Bedding plants (transplants) are a larger investment, so space them out properly, using almost the same spacing as if you were planting in a soil garden. The most important thing is to plant something and learn what works best for you.

# NO TOLERANCE FOR EYESORES

| NAME |
| --- |
| Paul Sorenson |
| **LOCATION** |
| Blaine, Minnesota |
| **NUMBER OF BALES** |
| 40 |
| **CROPS** |
| Cabbage, cucumbers, eggplant, green beans, herbs, impatiens, lettuce, peppers (hot and sweet), tomatoes |
| **SBG START DATE** |
| 2012 |
| **CHALLENGE** |
| Combine ornamentals and edibles without detracting from landscape |

PAUL SORENSON'S PARENTS had a bigger garden than he has now as an adult. Like many kids of gardening parents, Paul had a small plot of his own to plant and tend, although he remembers that about three-quarters of the way through the season, he'd lose enthusiasm. Yet the seeds of a love of gardening had been sown in Paul, and once he had a place of his own, he started a garden.

Paul's wife grew up on a farm in North Dakota, and her mother's garden was huge. Following her mother's example, at one point, Paul's wife had nine flower gardens. She loves ornamentals, whereas Paul is a vegetable and edibles gardener. In recent years, Paul has planted two impatiens flowers on the sides of some bales, and they do very well. In fact, Paul says, "They flourish so well, they take the whole bale over." Over the years, I've seen plenty of ways to dress up straw bales. Planting flowers on the sides of bales is a great way to add beauty to your bales. I once photographed Paul's bales with the impatiens in full bloom, and since then, I have used that image as my example of how great they can look!

*Opposite and above:* Paul's a natural when it comes to implementing systems and evaluating the soundness of any practice. His Straw Bale Garden is one of the most efficient and productive (and beautiful) gardens I have ever visited.

## Joel Says

Paul has nothing against black dirt, but he enjoys the benefits that accompany growing in straw bales. Paul says that a big part of the appeal is simply that it's "not traditional." Paul's foray into Straw Bale Gardening started with an article in the *Star Tribune*, the Minneapolis-based newspaper. Paul is wired to continuously look for ways to improve, so his wife knew that when growing in straw bales was mentioned, Paul's curiosity would be piqued. Paul read the article and began to evaluate the information. Intrigued, Paul didn't know how he could get a hold of the gentleman featured in the story. Later, he realized I lived in the Twin Cities. When he learned that I was giving a lecture close to his house, he drove to hear me speak. I've had hundreds of people come up to me after my presentations and ask questions or tell me about their gardens, but Paul was different. He was excited and very curious about things others never thought about.

*Above:* Peppers grow best when they don't get overwatered. The bales will drain excess rainfall or irrigation water, but avoiding too much water is a best practice.

*Opposite, bottom:* Paul's trellis wires are very taught. The white plastic electric-fence tensioners are designed to be twisted and to keep the wires tight.

## ENGINEERING A STRAW BALE GARDEN

Paul's garden setup is a "best practice." He followed the instructions laid out in my books to perfection. Paul has ample space on his property, so he has plenty of room for a large Straw Bale Garden. Paul has 4 rows of bales with 10 bales in each row for a total of 40 bales. His rows are straight as arrows, and his trellis wires are perfectly measured and tight as a drum.

The 180-foot perimeter of Paul's garden (50 feet by 40 feet) has a chain-link fence around it—it's electrified with three hot wires mounted on the chain link—to keep out all kinds of vegetable-loving wildlife, including raccoons, woodchucks, skunks, and deer. Paul says that "even the wild turkeys like to try to fly in!"

Paul has engineered a marvel of an irrigation system for his bales. He has set up his garden on two timers with four zones. Each timer can handle two zones, and Paul programs each row independently. He regulates the amount of water by row to ensure that each crop gets sufficient, but not too much, water.

Paul remembers, "Joel says that it's impossible to flood the bales. That's true. But with experience, I've learned that some crops need less water than one might think. It is important to not water too much—even with the good drainage." According to Paul, an example of a crop that doesn't need much water is tomatoes. To monitor the moisture conditions for his tomatoes, Paul checks by sticking his hand down in the bale and waters when needed rather than on a set schedule.

Paul varies what he grows each year for the fun of it. This year he's growing cucumbers, green beans, eggplant, peppers (both hot and sweet), leeks, and more than a dozen different tomatoes. Paul also grows "fantastic cabbage, broccoli, and kale" as well as lettuce and herbs, including basil, mint, and dill.

Paul's favorite variety of tomatoes changes each year. Lately, he's enjoyed harvesting Jet Star, Celebrity, and Big Girl. In 2017, the Whopper lived up to its name—Paul says it's quite large and grew bigger than a softball. Paul remarks, "For four years, I wasn't convinced of the results that the taste, with respect to tomatoes, was better. I'm very critical about that. This year I raised half my tomatoes in soil and half in bales. Now I can definitively say that the tomatoes grown in straw bales are just as good as the soil-grown tomatoes."

For a few years, Paul grew Yukon gold potatoes. This was interesting to try and worked fine. "You just reach down in the bale and pull out a potato!" Paul says.

Sweet corn is not suited to straw bales, so Paul grows that traditionally in soil. He is lucky that his soil is decent. After conducting numerous soil tests, the analysis is pretty good.

## PREFERENCE OVER NECESSITY

Many folks turn to Straw Bale Gardening when they encounter a major challenge with their property that traditional gardening cannot handle effectively. However, in Paul's case, he has no major barriers to effective traditional gardening—he's just a fan of Straw Bale Gardening. Here's why.

Paul says that one of the biggest advantages is the elevation of the gardening surface from the ground level to the top of the bale for easier gardening, which means no bending or stooping.

Another advantage is the addition of a trellis system over the straw bales. Having vines and veggies supported up and off the ground is a big factor for Paul. His plants are prone to fewer diseases up on the bales and on the trellis. Naturally, there are very few weeds.

Additionally, Paul says, "Straw Bale Gardening was interesting from just a novelty standpoint. It's great for compact gardening too. I'm growing quite a few things in a fairly small space."

My mother loved the bale garden, but she didn't initially like the way it looked. A few annual flowers tucked into the sides can change everything.

*Above:* (Before) Leave at least 4 feet between rows, but 5 or 6 is even better. Paul has lots of space, so he keeps his walkways plenty wide.

*Opposite:* (After) Paul lays down ground cloth and old plywood to prevent any weed growth between the rows. This also prevents muddy boots!

## THE SCIENCE OF CONDITIONING

For most gardeners, the conditioning process is unfamiliar territory, but to Paul it seemed pretty straightforward: "I'm an engineer—if there's a basis for it and it makes sense, then I know that there is a high likelihood of it working."

To prepare the bales for growing, Paul follows the recommended recipe and uses high-nitrogen fertilizer over 12 days. As Paul notes, "During conditioning, you are on a schedule, and you have to do something every day. That nitrogen accelerates the bacterial growth, and everything in the bale starts percolating. Essentially, you're growing in something that is on the path to being compost."

Paul did some experimenting with his bales during the conditioning process. He measured the temperature in each bale starting at day 1. Of course, the temperature inside the bale rises during conditioning, but Paul was interested in just how much it rises. He was surprised to note a variation in the rate and the peak temperature of his bales during conditioning. The peak temperatures were well over 100°F and ranged from 130° to 140°F. Paul loves seeing the high temperatures because he knows that the heat helps kill diseases and fungus. He notes, "I have a perpetual problem with fungus in my area, especially on tomatoes. I still try to guard against it, even growing in straw. So, anything I can do to thwart that is interesting to me."

Why was there a difference in the peak temperature of the bales during the conditioning process in Paul's garden? He suspects it has something to do with tightness of the bales, because "all my bales didn't come from the same source."

As Paul points out, straw is what is left over from a grain crop. Grain crops include rye, wheat, oats, barley, rice, and so forth, resulting in rye straws, wheat straw, oat straw, and others. There shouldn't be seeds in straw, as the seeds are harvested as part of the crop. As a result, the bales should be mostly sterile—no seeds—which results in less weeding. No seeds, no weeds.

## ADVICE FROM A PRO

Paul encourages folks who are curious about Straw Bale Gardening to find some straw and give it a try. For many potential gardeners, sourcing straw can be a challenge, so he emphasizes the importance of seeking out and following up on leads for bales. In some years, inexpensive bales have been difficult to source, and he has paid up to $7 or $8 per bale. Paul suggests starting with 5 or 10 bales.

Another thing Paul stresses is to not forget about sun. When vegetables don't perform well, it's important to consider their amount of sun exposure. "Make sure your bales are in full sun. That is always a success factor, and sometimes people forget about sunlight," he advises.

Paul fertilizes during the season as well. He uses 10-10-10 during the growing season, after the preliminary conditioning process is complete. He recognizes that tomatoes need a lot of phosphorus and potassium and factors that into his fertilizing regimen.

Perhaps Paul's most salient advice is to be observant. Manipulate some things when necessary, he suggests, and change it up and keep trying to optimize your efforts. I couldn't agree more.

*Above:* Paul's garden after planting. Note the tiny impatiens plugged into the sides of the bales. They'll put on a great show in a few weeks.

# FLYBY GARDENER

| NAME |
| --- |
| Chris Ashbach |
| **LOCATION** |
| Arden Hills, Minnesota |
| **NUMBER OF BALES** |
| 35 |
| **CROPS** |
| Beans, cabbage, cucumbers, herbs, peas, peppers, tomatoes |
| **SBG START DATE** |
| 2014 |
| **CHALLENGE** |
| No time for garden maintenance |
| **WEBSITES** |
| www.fourkidsandachicken.com www.livedan330.com |

AS A PILOT, Chris sometimes leaves town for a week or two at a time. With Straw Bale Gardening, his time investment is streamlined. He spends a weekend setting up the garden in the spring, followed by a week of 30 minutes a day prepping the bales and planting. For the rest of the growing season, Chris does a walk-through once every week or so and then starts harvesting. Chris loves the lesser time commitment of a Straw Bale Garden.

Chris grew up watching his dad tend a small vegetable garden. Chris remembers "pulling up carrots and ending up with a mouth full of dirt"—and then getting washed off under a hose. A lesson in cleaning the carrots with the hose followed. Vegetable gardening is something Chris knows well. However, once he encountered problems with the soil at his home, Chris decided to switch to growing flowers. After hearing about the Straw Bale Gardens method in detail at the state fairgrounds, Chris jumped in with both feet. He admits he was a bit skeptical but knew that "seeing is believing." The next year, Chris couldn't believe how well the plants did. He was amazed at this new gardening method and "quickly adopted it wholeheartedly for myself and my family."

Chris is a true Renaissance man. He not only is a vegetable gardener but keeps bees, flies jet airplanes professionally, and loves traveling. He is a nationally recognized blogger and speaker, an occasional adjunct professor, an accomplished photographer, a dad to four kids, and a husband. He still considers himself more of a flower gardener and has always liked having a neat look to his gardens. He loves having a fresh new palette each spring and arranges his bales differently each year. You'll see in his images how creatively he designs his gardens. "Straw Bale Gardening lets me design new garden concepts and patterns each year. I also love to use trellises that form shapes and tunnels to make the garden a living piece of art," says Chris. His kids and his wife also love the garden. Gardening is a great activity for a family, especially if you want to teach your kids about healthy eating and give them basic instructions on growing.

Once the garden trellises and irrigation systems were purchased years ago, the only additional expense for Chris is the bales in the spring. He feels that the cost is offset by the time it saves. Chris has recruited many people to try Straw Bale Gardening, including his father, his sister, and a couple of neighbors. Several friends have also started using the technique, and Chris has likely recruited hundreds of others to use the method by posting about his own garden on his popular blog, which is read by folks all around the world.

## AN EASY SOLUTION FOR POOR SOIL

After battling poor soil, Chris has spent the past few years incorporating huge volumes of decomposed straw into his old garden

*Above:* Chris's youngest, Estella Ann, has now become a gardener. The zucchini leaves are about half as tall as she is. Zucchini loves bales!

*Opposite:* Chris has a schedule that doesn't leave much time for garden maintenance. With traditional gardening, poor soil meant production was meager and weeds grew faster and bigger than the vegetables.

*Right:* Chris incorporated a few wire arches, made from concrete reinforcing wire panels that can be found at most lumber yards, in his garden.

*Opposite, top:* A low-maintenance garden can still give great results. Chris spent more time taking pictures than pulling weeds this season.

*Opposite, bottom:* The ability to seasonally change the garden layout by simply rearranging the bales allows Chris to be creative every spring.

beds. "A surprising benefit to the Straw Bale Garden is that it has helped me produce better soil for my traditional garden," Chris says. "Each year, I till in the remains of my straw bales to add rich organic material." Today, Chris has about one-quarter of his garden growing in the soil again. "Some things just do better for me in the soil than in the bales," Chris says.

### CROPS

This past year, Chris and the kids made an amazing gourd tunnel, a tomato tunnel, and a "wall of future pickles." The tunnels were made out of rewire (the rusty wire grids embedded in poured concrete), and the vines grew up and over the arched wire. As the fruit matured, all the beautiful gourds hung down at head height. They used the same method with tomatoes, and after harvesting over 500 pounds of tomatoes, they spent many hours turning them all into red sauce, ketchup, BBQ sauce, marinara, and bloody-mary mixer. They also turned the "future pickles" into actual pickles and canned enough of everything to carry them through until next summer's garden arrives. In addition, Chris grows squash and a variety of herbs. Since he is also a food blogger, Chris uses lots of fresh herbs as garnish when photographing dishes so they look professional.

### LIVEDAN330

Looking for advice on beekeeping, traveling, blogging, or social media, or wanting to try any one of a few thousand recipes? Check out Chris's websites, www.livedan330.com and www.fourkidsand achicken.com, where you will find thousands of ideas for dinner, cool places to travel, and funny, informative blog posts about a whole variety of topics. Chris also has a massive following on social-media platforms, including Pinterest.

## Joel Says

A few years ago, Chris and his father, Dan, showed up at an event I used to host every spring at the Minnesota State Fairgrounds called "Straw Bale Gardening Education Day." After hearing the presentation, they were committed to trying it for themselves.

# CLAY SOIL BLUES

| NAME | |
|---|---|
| Bill Maibach | |
| **LOCATION** | |
| Westerville, Ohio | |
| **NUMBER OF BALES** | |
| 54 | |
| **CROPS** | |
| Green beans, potatoes, tomatoes, and more | |
| **SBG START DATE** | |
| 2014 | |
| **CHALLENGE** | |
| Nutrient-deficient clay soil, drought | |

WHEN A GARDENER has mostly clay soil, the amount of rainfall in the spring can play a key role in the success of a garden. Every time it rains, it takes a week for the clay soil to dry out enough to work the soil or plant seeds. The seeds can easily mold or rot in standing water, and young plants take a while to grow big enough to start helping draw moisture out of the soil through transpiration.

With straw bales, there is no waiting for the soil to dry out. Bill can simply pick a day when he wants to plant and plan accordingly. He loves the fact that he pulls almost no weeds anymore, and he hasn't used his rototiller since he started the Straw Bale Gardens technique. "I'm 66 years old, and ground work is more difficult now than when I was younger; that's one more reason I am enjoying the whole process much more," Bill says.

Bill read an article about the Straw Bale Gardens method a few years back and immediately purchased the book. The only skepticism he had was in his own ability to recreate the process that the book had laid out for him. I have seen many Straw Bale Gardens, and I must say that, as his images here attest, Bill has created a textbook example of the system defined in the book. He obviously was destined for success, but even while his friends and family showed interest in this new project, they also were a bit skeptical, not really understanding how it was possible.

An Ohio farm boy, Bill learned the rigors of growing a large vegetable garden very early in his youth. With Bill having 11 siblings and lots of aunts, uncles, cousins, and friends, the farm garden had a big production goal every year. His family maintained a large regular garden in addition to an even larger truck garden. They used farm equipment to plant crops, including those that required lots of space, such as corn, beans, and vining crops such as potatoes. They had great soil on the farm back then, but Bill's current residence in

*Left:* Bill's garden started out much smaller, but once his neighbors joined the effort, it grew much bigger the second year.

*Opposite, top:* It takes a little planning, effort, and a few bucks to get set up the first year, but after that first year it is simple.

## Joel Says

It isn't easy or free to get a setup in place like Bill has in his pictures, but once it is set up, it is easy to care for and harvest. The setup should only take one big effort, because it can be left in position for future years. Simply fork out the old bales and roll in the new ones. With that done, the spring preparation is complete, and conditioning can begin.

Westerville, Ohio, isn't nearly as productive. As a matter of fact, the heavy clay appeared only to favor the weeds that seemed to always outpace any seeds planted in his gardens.

Bill is a believer in organic production and loves what most of us love about our vegetable gardens. Fresh produce isn't comparable to what you can get at even the most local grocery stores. The flavor of homegrown vegetables is really about the proximity to the table where they will be eaten. The closer the better!

### A GROUP EFFORT

During the first year, his neighbors merely observed his success, but they have now joined forces, and after expanding the garden twice, they are up to 54 bales and are feeding the whole neighborhood. Bill says, "I love to walk through the garden most evenings and pick a lone weed, tie up a plant, or make a slight adjustment. Overall, the time to garden this way versus the old way isn't even comparable; it's at least 75 percent less work, and it doesn't actually cost any more in the long run."

What is most amazing to Bill is how productive his second-year bales are: his potatoes grow even better in them than the first year's did. He is correct in his observations, and it's likely you will realize the same thing. Never discard the partially decomposed straw bales. They are nicely decomposed inside, and while they will not heat up again like a first-season bale does, they have more available nutrients and hold moisture very well.

*Above:* Take note of the fancy hard-pipe PVC irrigation line above that feeds each of the eight rows. No hoses means no tripping. I'm jealous.

*Left:* Bill can step out to the garden and harvest dinner with fewer steps and in less time than he would normally spend at the grocery.

*Opposite:* A few second-season bales among the new bales and a fenced planter box filled with third-year bales planted with potatoes.

Bill grows about every vegetable you can think of, but he says, "My potatoes, tomatoes, and green beans seem to do the best." Bill is experimenting this year with a planter box of sorts, made with a fenced-in area 2 feet by 2 feet by 25 feet. He filled it up with third-year bales and says, "All I can say is *wow!* The plants are growing like crazy."

## CREATING A BED FOR BULBS

| | |
|---|---|
| **NAME** | |
| Juan Manuel Vasquez | |
| **LOCATION** | |
| Buenos Aires, Argentina | |
| **NUMBER OF BALES** | |
| 30 | |
| **CROPS** | |
| Lettuce, saffron crocus, tomatoes, and more | |
| **SBG START DATE** | |
| 2014 | |
| **CHALLENGE** | |
| Large-scale planting, hard, dry soil | |

PLANTING BULBS IN HARD, DRY SOIL is backbreaking work. It means digging individual holes for every bulb in the spring and then digging up each bulb in the fall for storage. A new enterprise growing bulbs in such conditions was going to be extremely difficult to pull off at any large scale. The Straw Bale Gardens method would work well, by Juan's analysis, to solve his soil problems and moisture issues, in addition to making bulbs easy to plant and harvest. Juan knew he could have an almost endless supply of straw bales at almost no cost. He also found a number of sellers who offered the newer-style large square bales that measure 3 feet by 4 feet by 6 feet. The large bales would work well and would be more economical, and if they could be cut in half to a height of 18 inches, they would be perfect.

Juan grew up watching his grandmother grow flowers on her balcony, but he didn't really have many opportunities to grow vegetables in his youth. Most people in Buenos Aires do not have access to much green space, and gardening isn't something most people consider to be a possibility. Since Juan has had some professional success, he was able to get a place with some land for growing.

The soil texture at Juan's property near Buenos Aires isn't very amenable to growing vegetables, and he also has problems maintaining the soil moisture to keep the garden growing well. Juan says, "It dries out quickly and requires much more attention than I can give it; I travel often and can't do maintenance every day." In addition to these issues, he fights weeds that make gardening very painful, especially for his lower back. With so many difficulties, his new idea to grow bulbs was a tall order until he discovered Straw Bale Gardening. Juan had no difficulties finding many sources for smaller bales of straw, as he is an architect with a company that builds structures made with straw bales in the walls as insulation and structural elements. When Juan ran across Straw Bale Gardening, his first thought was, "What a great way to use all of the bales left over from projects . . . that didn't meet the quality standards for moisture content and compression." He now has set up a small Straw Bale Garden for vegetables, with several bales for crocuses. He has plans to expand as well.

## GROWING SAFFRON

Juan also happens to love Spanish paella and likes to make it taste authentic when he cooks. This requires an expensive spice called saffron, which is so valuable that it is worth more than gold by weight. Saffron is used in many other foods around the world. In India, it goes in rice, sweets, and ice cream. In Saudi Arabia, it goes in Arabic coffee. In northern Italy, it's an essential ingredient in risotto. Sweden bakes a famous bread with it, and in Spain, it goes in paella.

*Opposite: Crocus sativus linnaeus* corms will produce a single gram of saffron with every 150 flowers. You'll need tweezers and lots of patience.

## Joel Says

Cutting large bales in half with a chainsaw is much easier than it may sound. I always suggest borrowing the neighbor's chainsaw, because it does tend to gum up the chain and the insides a little. Moving around such large bales can be the most difficult aspect of using them. Once the bales are dropped in place, you can still move them, but you might need five neighbors and a block and tackle since they are heavy and awkward. This method also works well with large round bales as well.

Saffron is expensive for a reason. It takes 150 *Crocus sativus linnaeus* flowers to produce just 1 single gram, or .035 ounces—the same weight as one single cotton ball. A single gram of saffron sells for between $40 and $55, and many recipes call for 1 or 2 grams of saffron. That is some expensive risotto!

Juan, like any good entrepreneur, was thinking about turning a buck into 20 bucks. Growing 400 saffron corms in one large bale would yield 400 flowers in year one, 1,200 in year two, and 2,400 by year three. After that point, the bale is likely done producing and the corms should be dug up and moved into a new bale. Using these calculations, each large bale could produce $1,466 in its life cycle. The problem is that someone must harvest the three tiny stigmas with tweezers from inside every tiny flower. It is very labor intensive but something anyone can grow, since it is rather easy to produce.

Starting small, Juan planted a few bales and has reported back that it works fantastically and that he is well on the way to having his own saffron-production plantation.

### CROPS

Tomatoes and lettuce are two of Juan's favorites, but a large selection of vegetables is growing in his garden. Juan says, "I love to cook, and of course, fresh vegetables make any recipe much better." Juan says he loves gardening, and like most people, he wishes he had time to do more of it. He also loves to teach his kids about gardening as well, so Juan wanted to teach his kids about gardening, and planting this garden at home was something he had planned to do someday. Discovering Straw Bale Gardening inspired him to leap into a garden the next spring. The saffron part of the story only came along later that summer, when Juan was faced with purchasing the expensive saffron spice for one of his family's paella picnics. Growing saffron in bulk quickly went from idea to reality. He planted that fall, and the following spring the crocus popped out of the bales, flowering right on schedule in the fall. Corms each produce one flower and several new corms to take its place the next season.

### URBAN FOOD SECURITY

Juan worked with 12 Argentinean city mayors to create the framework of a conference that would work to develop a program based around the Milan Urban Food Policy Pact (MUFPP) for these cities. He invited me to speak to that conference and work to develop a program that would utilize the Straw Bale Gardens method to implement some of the vegetable-growing opportunities for poor urban dwellers.

*Top:* Use a large square bale cut in half with a chainsaw—the result is a half bale 18 inches high, 4 feet wide, and 5 feet long.

*Bottom:* Condition the bale, make a hole with a stick, drop the crocus corm into the hole about 3 to 4 inches deep, and just wait until it flowers.

The program continues to grow and expand, with many new cities around the world adopting the MUFPP for themselves. The pact states that cities that host over half the world's population have a strategic role to play in developing sustainable food systems and promoting healthy diets. While every city is different, they are all centers of economic, political, and cultural innovation and manage vast public resources, infrastructure, investments, and expertise, so they do have a significant role in helping solve this urban food-security issue. I will do my best to continue to try to convince them that the Straw Bale Gardens method is definitely a viable option that, when scaled up, can easily serve as a reproducible, predictable, and understandable concept.

*Left:* Whether 50 crocus in one small bale or 400 in a large half bale—the number of flowers will increase every year with no additional effort.

*Bottom, left:* The harvest is really the hardest part of growing saffron; a thimbleful of those beautiful red stigmas are the only crop.

*Bottom, right:* Kids love to garden alongside their parents, and it may be the most valuable life skill you ever get to teach a child.

# EXTREME SOLUTION FOR A SHORT SEASON

| NAME |
| --- |
| Char Ouellette |
| **LOCATION** |
| Salem, Oregon |
| **NUMBER OF BALES** |
| 15 |
| **CROPS** |
| Beans, cucumbers, peas, peppers, squash, tomatoes |
| **SBG START DATE** |
| 2016 |
| **CHALLENGE** |
| High-desert conditions |

THE HIGH DESERT is a notoriously difficult place to garden. Gardeners in this part of Oregon face three challenges: climate, water, and soil. The climate offers extreme day and night temperature changes, extreme and rapid weather changes, and an exceptionally short growing season. During conditioning, when the bales start to decompose, they heat up and stay warm for the next 6 weeks. At peak temperatures during the conditioning process, the bales can get as warm as 150°F for the first couple of weeks. The bales then quickly drop below 105°F, at which time they can be planted or seeded. Loving the heat generated by the decomposition, the new seedlings and transplants grow faster than any those planted in the cold soil. Should a late-spring frost come along, a sheet of plastic can be pulled over the top of the bale to create a mini greenhouse. Holding in the heat, the plastic is sufficient to protect new transplants down to very cold temps.

After getting married, Char and her husband purchased 5 acres of land in the Willamette Valley of Oregon. In the middle of USDA Hardiness Zone 6, Willamette Valley is oceanic with dry, warm, cloudless summers. Excited to start gardening, Char picked what she thought would be a perfect spot for her garden down in the field . . . except she forgot about access to water. Unsure of the tools she needed to be successful, Char questioned whether gardening in the clay soil was even worth it. Char remembers, "I was hauling water down our hill in buckets, and I think we got a couple ears of corn that first year."

In 2014, Char and her husband moved to the high desert of central Oregon. The high desert is drastically different from the Mediterranean-like Willamette Valley. With an average rainfall of less than 5 inches during the growing season, water was a concern. Char had no idea how to garden in the high desert or even if she could actually get a vegetable garden to grow there.

Back in the Valley, Char had a friend who had started a Straw Bale Garden. Desperate for a way to make gardening more viable in her area, Char decided to do a little research on the method. She bought the book *Straw Bale Gardens* and read up on the details. It sounded perfect for a short growing season, but lots of things can sound good. Would it work for her?

## SETUP

Char and her husband sourced straw bales and set about conditioning them in their first spring in the desert. Char says she understood the concept of Straw Bale Gardening after reading the book, but still she wondered how the plants would actually perform without soil. She remembers, "My husband was skeptical of the process, and then one day while we were conditioning the bales, he stuck his

*Opposite:* Tucked between large pine trees in a spot that gets a good amount of sunlight, Char's garden has become her pride and joy.

## Joel Says

Char's first experience gardening in the clay of her Willamette Valley field was frustrating, to say the least. But it sums up the experience that many first-time gardeners have when they attempt a traditional garden on an impossible site.

## Joel Says

Because they raise the work surface, bales eliminate hours of stooping and kneeling. Like many gardeners, Char doesn't like the back pain that often follows a day of working in the garden. Getting down on the ground or bending down all day can leave one reaching for a bottle of painkillers the next morning. Gardeners keep the masseurs in business during the growing season every summer!

*Top:* Gardeners often discover that they can now grow things in bales that were not hardy in their climate when they were growing in soil.

*Bottom:* Use sticks to guide peas up to the trellis wires. I like to use dogwood branches right after I prune them in the spring.

barbecue thermometer into a bale." It was a cool day, and he was shocked to see that the temperature inside the bale was well over 100°F. With the trellis system above the bales, Char and her husband can easily run out and cover their crops with plastic in the event of freezing temperatures, which can happen anytime—even during the summer months.

During that first summer with their Straw Bale Garden, Char and her husband learned the method could hold its own against the extremes of the high desert. Many benefits presented themselves. "It's not just one thing—it's multiple things," Char explains. "The bales in their rows look neat and tidy. They generate heat to keep the garden wonderfully warm when temperatures plummet. There's no need for extra soil, no more rotating crops, and the bales naturally raise the beds."

## CROPS

The short growing season makes gardening difficult in the high desert. Freezing temperatures can nip a crop without much warning. Char has been amazed by the crops of tomatoes, cucumbers, and peppers they have consistently gotten with the Straw Bale Gardens method over the last 3 years. She had kale that carried over to the next year, even after having been completely covered by snow for 3 months.

Char adds, "The flavor of the tomatoes is so much better than store bought. It is so rewarding to grow the food that you eat, knowing what went into the food that you've grown and how healthy it is for your family. It's exciting to see your little flowers turn into veggies. It's a nice sense of accomplishment and good exercise as well."

## Joel Says

Once folks receive a good explanation about the fungi and bacteria quickly converting the straw into compost (or early-stage soil), curiosity gives way to understanding. But really, it's only after people try it themselves that folks become completely convinced. Don't be surprised when a stranger pulls up in their car, hops out, and says, "I've been driving by your garden all summer—can you give me a tour? I just have to ask you some questions." A version of this scenario happens to everyone who starts a Straw Bale Garden, so be prepared.

### SISTERS GARDEN CLUB GARDEN TOUR

Straw Bale Gardens attract attention, and neighbors and friends are naturally curious. This past summer, Char was surprised when she was asked to participate in the Sisters Garden Club Garden Tour. Nearly 500 gardeners toured Char's Straw Bale Garden. Char says that many were fascinated, and nearly all of them asked, "Where is the soil?!" Explaining how the process really works gives every Straw Bale Gardener the opportunity to become a teacher.

*Above, left:* The colored bark mulch Char has used to prevent weeds between her rows of bales really makes the garden look tidy.

*Above, right:* The beautiful, bright-red tomato cages used here are attractive and very useful; just make certain they are securely fastened.

# SANDY SOIL & RAMPANT WILDLIFE

| NAME | |
|---|---|
| Joni Graves | |
| **LOCATION** | |
| Spring Green, Wisconsin | |
| **NUMBER OF BALES** | |
| 40 | |
| **CROPS** | |
| Basil, beans, cucumbers, potatoes, squash, sweet potatoes, tomatoes | |
| **SBG START DATE** | |
| 2013 | |
| **CHALLENGE** | |
| Sandy soil, moles, and black walnut trees | |

SOIL PROBLEMS STOP a lot of gardeners in their tracks before they can even get started. For Joni Graves, the almost pure-sand soil at her property in Wisconsin makes a traditional garden unworkable. Add to this a large labor of moles who make quick work of tunneling through the sand to reach the plants, as well as the presence of black walnut trees, and the outlook for growing vegetables was poor.

Then, one day in 2013, Joni was listening to the *Larry Meiller Show* on Wisconsin Public Radio, and she caught my interview with Larry about Straw Bale Gardening. Thinking of her struggles with sand and moles, she loved the SBG idea right away and decided that it was time to try gardening again—but differently this time. Joni's husband and stepdaughter, an accomplished gardener in her own right, were very skeptical about this new idea. Joni says, "I went ahead anyway, and it was fantastic—both the process, which was very creative, and the results, which were delicious."

Quickly winning over her skeptics and soon many others, Joni is now a full-fledged supporter of the Straw Bale Gardening method. She has even joined our Certified Straw Bale Gardening Instructors program and is listed on our website. She has received rave reviews from several people who have heard Joni, the Hater of Woodchucks, give a presentation about Straw Bale Gardening. One of her friends left her a review that says, "I watched with great interest when Joni plunged into her first straw bale project about 5 years ago. It was a totally new idea to me, and I guess I was obviously skeptical. Consider me a convert now!" Joni has already converted many friends and neighbors to the Straw Bale Gardening, and she doesn't intend to stop growing in bales anytime soon.

*Above:* A network of soaker hoses attached to a timer eliminates much of the SBG watering labor for Joni. But she does keep a ready supply of water buckets warming for spot watering as needed.

*Opposite:* The sections of large-diameter logs stacked soldier-style around the perimeter of Joni's gardens have the practical purpose of keeping out small animals. But they also make a lovely design statement.

## Joel Says

For many gardeners in Wisconsin who have black walnut trees on their property, the probability of ever having a vegetable garden is bleak. Black walnut (*Juglans nigra*) produces the allelochemical called juglone, which is emitted from its roots into the soil around the root zone to kill competitive vegetation. This chemical inhibits the growth of some species greatly while others not at all. Allelopathy isn't completely understood, but for anyone who has ever tried to grow flowers or vegetables anywhere near a big black walnut tree, the effects are understood completely. No matter the contamination, when it comes to dealing with soil, straw bales offer an affordable solution above the soil line. Take tomatoes, for example, the roots of which can grow down through the bale. Were they to grow into the soil, they would need to get at least a few inches deep into the soil to absorb the juglone, but they don't. In time, a tree's roots would likely grow up into a permanent raised bed and cause the same issue.

*Top:* Joni's gardens are a wealth of creative ideas, from soda-can drainage outlets to plant labels and root shields. Even the crop selection (onions!) is a joy to study.

*Bottom:* Draping shading fabric over trellis supports on hot summer days provides welcome relief for the garden. Extending the fabric past the bales makes a lovely shaded area for the gardeners too.

### JONI'S GARDEN

"As much as I loved my grandparents, as a kid I thought gardening was kind of boring and an incredible amount of work!" Joni says emphatically. "Rototilling, weeding on my hands and knees in the hot sun? No thanks. Those things aren't necessary with Straw Bale Gardening." Joni's garden has grown to over 40 bales and has to be one of the most photogenic Straw Bale Gardens I've seen. She installs a lovely shade cloth over the top of her trellis work when the summer sun and temperatures max out in July and August in Wisconsin.

"I don't even own a rototiller!" Joni says, laughing. During a lovely summer afternoon, you may find Joni reading a book out in her Straw Bale Garden. Now, isn't that is the way to grow vegetables?

### CROPS

Like Joni's grandfather taught her, the best vegetables are fresh vegetables. Joni claims he was known for bringing a pot of water to a boil before he went to pick the sweetcorn—he liked it fresh. She's the same way: Fresh is best, so pick it and try to eat it the same day. She grows basil, beans, cucumbers, squash, tomatoes, sweet potatoes, potatoes, and many more veggies, and she shares lots of her fresh crops with friends as well. One of her friends who hasn't yet taken up gardening herself says, "While Joni hasn't yet inspired me enough to grow my own garden, I have learned so much from her. The main thing I've learned is that I really love being her friend!"

## Joel Says

Let Straw Bale Gardening change your life, or the life of someone you know who could use a lift. I can tell you that Joni isn't the first to tell me about how their Straw Bale Garden accomplished this. People who grow a Straw Bale Garden for the first time are often very inspired by their success and delighted by the friendly inquiries from neighbors and friends who are truly interested. Almost a byproduct are the actual vegetables that can inspire a healthier diet and may be the push someone needs each day to get outside and exercise just a little bit. The best stories I've heard from Straw Bale Gardeners are not about the giant tomato they grew but rather about how it was a fun and fulfilling experience. I recall not long ago a woman telling me her father had recently passed away, but for the past two years they had been growing a Straw Bale Garden together at his place, and how fun it was, how many phone calls they had to talk about it, and how they looked forward to it together. I could see what it meant to her as she teared up telling me the story. It seems like a sales pitch, but I have seen it actually change the lives of many people. If you know someone who could use a good thing in their life, suggest to them that they try growing a Straw Bale Garden, or better yet, help them get one set up for the first time. Then observe the changes for yourself over the following year or two.

Joni recalls, "My first year of Straw Bale Gardening coincided with a trip we took to England. I was away for a couple of weeks, and when we got back in mid-July, I could not believe the profusion of produce. To a new gardener, it was amazing!"

## CHANGE YOUR LIFE?

Joni's instructor listing on our website is inspiring. Here is what it says:

When Joel Karsten interviewed me in February 2016, he asked why I had been attracted to Straw Bale Gardening and I told him, "Because I wanted to change my life."

I didn't know that when I listened to him on Wisconsin Public Radio in 2013, but I quickly knew that I wanted to create a Straw Bale Garden. I had never had anything more than a small container garden before, but I started with nearly 30 bales and it was transformative.

The second year I expanded my garden to almost 40 bales and I created an installation inspired by Fritz Haeg's *Foraging Circle* at the Minneapolis Sculpture Garden.

My recent SBG gardens have been more rampant, but no less delightful and very productive.

One of the things that I love the most about working in my garden is the endless opportunity for creative problem solving—so, it feeds the mind as well as the body.

Joni uses and "all of the above" critter-management strategy in her rural Wisconsin setting. It even includes the selective use of electric fencing to ward off deer.

Joni's SBG, boasting 40 bales, is one of the best-conceived and most beautiful SBGs I have seen.

# CHAPTER 4

# SOLUTIONS FOR SCHOOLS, BUSINESSES, AND COMMUNITIES

IF YOU HAVE EVER BEEN a member of a community garden, you know that the members all show up for the first day of work in the garden and again when harvesting begins, but on weeding day, it can be hard to get them to answer their phones. Whenever groups of people collaborate on any project, it seems a small number of people end up carrying more weight than others in the group.

I've heard hundreds of stories of community gardens, including church gardens, school gardens, corporate gardens, restaurant gardens, housing-complex gardens, clinic gardens, library gardens, preschool gardens, retirement-home gardens, and others. These groups have sometimes converted traditional gardens over to bales, while others initially started with bales. But they all have one thing in common, and that's bales.

Some of these groups are made up of very young, new gardeners just learning about growing seeds for the first time, while other groups are all seasoned gardeners growing in bales because bending over to ground level isn't so easy anymore. Take a look through the example gardens I selected for this chapter and keep the Straw Bale Garden option in mind the next time you are trying to reach your fellow community-garden members on weeding day.

Johnny, one of the younger volunteers with the Kearny, New Jersey, community garden, is checking to see if the bales are fully cooked. See pages 104 to 107.

# CROP-ROTATION BLUES

| | |
|---|---|
| **NAME** | |
| Perry White | |
| **LOCATION** | |
| Marion, Illinois | |
| **NUMBER OF BALES** | |
| 25 | |
| **CROPS** | |
| Beans, cucumbers, peppers, squash, tomatoes | |
| **SBG START DATE** | |
| 2016 | |
| **CHALLENGE** | |
| No crop rotation possible in a small community garden | |

CROP ROTATION IS AN IRONCLAD TENET of smart gardening. Any gardener who has paid minimal attention to the pursuit knows how important it is to shift crops around from year to year to prevent yield from diminishing. The reason, most assume, is that each individual crop is unique in what it takes from and puts into the soil. If you plant heavy nitrogen feeders in the same spot year after year, they will deplete the nitrogen in that patch and eventually will no longer thrive there. So you should alternate planting them with nitrogen-fixing plants, which add nitrogen rather than consume it. This makes sense. But there is another important reason to rotate your crops: disease and pests. Most of the worst plant diseases and infesters do not travel far. Tomato blight, for example, resides in the soil, where it attacks any tomato that is planted in the vicinity year after year. Most gardeners move their tomatoes around the garden every year, but what happens when the physical conditions of your garden don't give you the flexibility to rotate? Perry White, a residential-complex community gardener from Illinois, faced this problem.

The tiny community garden he shares with other residents of his complex grows in the same exact small spaces every year. Once blight shows up on tomatoes, the spores continue to live on in the leaf litter that gets worked into the soil. Any tomatoes planted into that spore-infested soil are likely to get spores splashed onto leaves from watering or rain, and that reintroduces the blight the next season. The same goes for insects that remain year to year in the topsoil. When these insects are offered the food source they like best every year, they can reproduce and overpopulate, and the consequences can be devastating.

When Perry started participating in the community-garden plot several years ago, he didn't have much initial success. He said, "Between the squirrels, the blight, and issues with adequate watering, I didn't harvest much at all for the first couple of years."

Then, as he was searching for something on YouTube, up popped one of my videos about the Straw Bale Gardens method. Perry said, "I have a bad back, and running the rototiller isn't my favorite job either, so this looked like a great option for our community gardens." He decided to get more information, so he bought a copy of *Straw Bale Gardens Complete* and put together a plan for the next spring.

In a Straw Bale Garden, you can plant crops in the exact same location year after year without rotating crops as long as you do rotate the "soil" by introducing new bales every year or two. The ability to elevate the plant roots in a bale means any insects remaining from last season are 20 inches beneath the newly planted seeds and out of reach of new transplants in the top of the bale. The soil around the bales cannot splash high enough, even during a heavy rainfall, to transport spores to the leaves of tomatoes planted up on top. As

*Above:* Yes, there are bales underneath those vines. It is common to get so much growth that you can't easily walk around in the garden.

*Opposite:* Several smaller plots make up the community garden at this residential complex—the residents appreciate the food grown by a few but shared with everyone.

## Joel Says

I recently contacted Perry to ask a few questions for this profile, and sure enough, he had the University of Illinois Extension Service specialist over at his house at that exact moment. He was teaching her the details of the Straw Bale Gardens method, and they both spoke to me on speakerphone. She was excited about the success the community gardens at the Marion complex had this year, and was excited to learn all about using straw bales to grow vegetables.

long as you don't touch the soil and then touch your plants, the spores will be left without a host for a year. Give the soil a few years without adding new spore-infested leaf litter and the spores will all be dead, making the soil once again "clean" enough for planting.

Perry convinced his fellow community gardeners to try the Straw Bale Gardens method, and the experiment began.

Skepticism from many others in the housing complex was rampant, according to Perry. The truth is that Perry was just a bit of a skeptic too as he started the conditioning, and was concerned that the bales weren't heating up very quickly. He said he learned later that he was likely using too much water, complicated by the fact that in the spring, water from a hose can be too cold. The cold water chills the bacteria and thus keeps the bales cool. He told me, "I emailed you, and you advised me to only use a gallon per bale per day, and after that, they heated up quickly."

Perry has been a real leader for the Marion Housing Authority complex. The complex is home to lots of senior citizens, and Perry said they love the raised height. Sometimes they even run their scooters or wheelchairs right between the rows of bales. The produce from the garden is important to many of the residents, who often

*Right:* Fellow residents volunteer in the garden and help with whatever work needs it. A little weeding between the rows of bales is the worst job.

*Bottom, left:* A community garden that is built at ground level, without curbing but with solid ground between rows, allows easy access for all.

*Bottom, right:* Anyone using a wheelchair or a scooter can still drive right up and down the rows of the garden and become an active participant.

stretch to make groceries last through each month. Perry said, "The main purpose when we started was to bring folks together, and I can honestly say that it has done that. It gives them a reason to get out of their apartments and take a stroll to look at the gardens and maybe bring home some really nice produce."

Perry has spearheaded the project, but many others have contributed their time as well. He emphasizes, "It's been a real joy to see the public housing tenants get so excited while watching all the stages of growth in the gardens. I garden and I volunteer because I enjoy helping people who need help and because they appreciate it. They thank me daily for helping them and for setting up the Straw Bale Gardens."

## CROPS

Tomatoes, of course, are the one crop everyone seems to love, so they have lots of those planted. Perry told me, "The Juliet tomato was a big hit and [the plants] have been heavy producers." In addition, they plant squash, cucumbers, green beans, peppers, turnips, kale, basil, and collard greens, and Perry reports that everything seems to grow very well. He hopes to expand the garden and plant different varieties next year. Perry has a brother-in-law who is now excited about doing his own Straw Bale Garden next year, and he always plants a big garden, so he really likes this method. He tells me that several others have said they also want to try it next year. He said that with a 25-bale garden, he estimates he spent about $50 more this year using bales than before using bales, but the difference is "a great tradeoff for rototilling and stooping over."

Peppers are a popular crop for all gardeners, and they grow well in bales. These are jalapeño plants, which average about 20 peppers.

## Joel Says

I don't know Perry personally, but we've talked on the phone and emailed back and forth for a while, and he strikes me as a really good fella with a big heart. We should all consider helping someone or sharing our bounty with people who need help. Maybe that means planting an extra bale with a couple of plants and committing to donating all the production from that bale or from a few bales to a local food shelf. Find someone who could use a little extra help and offer them a box of your surplus harvest. It's nice to share a favorite recipe to go with the box of vegetables you drop off as well, because it is very possible that the person who receives those fresh vegetables may not even know what they are. You'd be surprised how many zucchini get peeled and sliced onto salads because they were mistaken for cucumbers. If you cook with fresh vegetables all the time, you may take for granted that others will know what you know. That isn't always the case. If you have children, let them participate in the growing and in the giving. While this will cost you very little money, this simple act will make a bigger impression than the most expensive gift you ever buy for your son or daughter.

# STRAW BALES GROW A BUSINESS DOWN UNDER

| NAME | |
|---|---|
| Tracey Sidwell | |
| **LOCATION** | |
| Tooradin, Australia | |
| **NUMBER OF BALES** | |
| 36 | |
| **CROPS** | |
| Cucumbers, lettuce, peppers, squash, tomatoes, and more | |
| **SBG START DATE** | |
| 2013 | |
| **CHALLENGE** | |
| Finding a more economical way to garden | |
| **WEBSITE** | |
| www.balegrow.com.au | |
| **FACEBOOK** | |
| BaleGrow | |

WATCHING BOTH OF HER grandmothers spending long hours tending gardens, Tracey Sidwell grew up with a perception of gardening as a massively time-consuming and laborious effort. Yet she also recalled how much she loved the convenience and superior flavor of homegrown vegetables. As a young newlywed living in her native Australia, she very much wanted to grow a garden of her own and emulate her grandmothers, who were "quite keen gardeners." In her first attempts at grandmother-style gardening, she failed numerous times, eventually contenting herself with small herb gardens. Because she was not interested in spending every precious free minute in her schedule tending a garden to make it successful, Tracey abandoned both her dreams of a beautiful vegetable garden and her desire to continue her grandmothers' passion for growing.

Then, when a friend invited Tracey to a garden-club meeting at the local elementary school her children attended, Tracey agreed to tag along, intending only to listen. However, after seeing the excitement and enthusiasm of the children at the prospect of a school garden, Tracey quickly changed her mind and pitched right in. Remembering the days gardening with her grandmothers, Tracey recognized that starting her own veggie patch was an important experience she wanted for her children. Convinced there had to be more modern and less laborious methods for gardening, Tracey began to research how to start a garden with minimal cost and time.

One day, Tracey's husband came home from work and shared a story of an interesting delivery of straw bales he had encountered on his route. The bales themselves were not extraordinary, but their intended purpose was very intriguing. After making his delivery, Tracey's husband was surprised to learn the load of straw bales was ordered for gardening to grow potatoes.

The timing was impeccable, as Tracey had committed herself to finding a way to garden using less time, effort, and money. Suspecting the method might make gardening a less demanding endeavor, Tracey did her homework and read a copy of *Straw Bale Gardens*. Learning about the Straw Bale Gardens method was a "light-bulb moment" for Tracey. "Even if it doesn't work, I can cut the strings, spread the straw around as mulch, and forget it ever happened!"

Tracey quickly did the math. Straw Bale Gardening was a fraction of the cost of the other main option she had considered, building raised beds. For the price of the bales and conditioning agents, Straw Bale Gardening offered a low-investment solution, in both time and money, while promising tremendous results. So she decided to give it a shot.

*Above:* Tracey's business has now evolved into teaching Straw Bale Gardening to children at preschools and kindergartens. They absorb her lessons like sponges.

*Opposite:* A mother of four children and a native Australian, Tracey Sidwell lives in the idyllic town of Tooradin. With a population of just over 1,300, Tooradin lies on the intercostal waterway called Western Port Bay, just southeast of Melbourne in southern Australia.

Kids love to garden with their parents, but tiny feet can easily step on plants in a soil garden, which can be hard to deal with. Bales love kids!

## YEAR ONE

With four children, Tracey was not excited about eliminating play space in the backyard with a big garden, so she decided that a front-yard garden would work best. When asked how Straw Bale Gardening went after her first year, Tracey responded, "I loved it, and the kids loved it!"

With instant success the first year, Tracey considered herself a pro at this new technique by year two. "I was amazed—along with the rest of my extended family—that I could grow anything!"

Anyone who has planted vegetable seeds and transplanted seedlings in rows of straw bales can vouch for getting a few funny looks from neighbors and passersby. As luck would have it, the decision to install a front-yard garden had a positive social impact on the whole family. Meeting neighbors they otherwise never knew existed was a pleasant surprise, and Tracey realized the bales were magnets for conversation. "Almost everyone would stop and chat about my bales. They were amazed at what I was doing and how well it worked. I feel a great deal of satisfaction and pride when I see something I planted growing right in front of my eyes. And it truly warms my heart to see my kids outside in the garden, picking vegetables for that night's dinner. Knowing that our garden harvest can nourish their little bodies . . . it never gets old!"

## CROPS

Tracey has great luck with many varieties of lettuce, beets, spinach, and Asian greens. She also grows zucchini and other squash, tomatoes, eggplant, cucumbers, pumpkins, and potatoes. She has grown many different varieties of annual flowers in her bales as well.

## TURNING A PASSION INTO A BUSINESS

Tracey worked hard to learn about Straw Bale Gardening all on her own. After mastering the method, she wanted to spare other busy moms and curious gardeners from having to do the same research. This notion of wanting to save time inspired yet another light-bulb moment—the idea to create an organic bale-conditioning agent called BaleGrow. By eliminating the required step of researching the Straw Bale Gardens method, Tracey's BaleGrow offers people a shortcut with which they can easily start their own Straw Bale Garden.

Educating people about growing their own food has now become a passion for Tracey and her family. They have introduced the BaleGrow product all over their region of Australia and demonstrated the Straw Bale Gardening technique to thousands of people. Equipped with a long list of successful gardeners and projects, Tracey loves persuading traditional gardeners to try Straw Bale Gardens.

Although she has built a thriving business selling her BaleGrow product in Australia, Tracey still encounters some occasional skepticism from traditional gardeners when she attends garden expos and presents at garden clubs. Adept at handling naysayers, she knows the best way to convince doubters is physical proof. Even more effective than showing images of hundreds of beautiful gardens, Tracey brings an actual straw bale complete with healthy plants to every event. The conversation quickly shifts from "Does that really work?" to "How can I get started?"

Tracey takes pride in her work of making the process of growing a garden easier. "I feel like I am having a positive impact on so many others and on the environment around me."

## BALEGROW FOR KIDS

Now that she has transformed her passion for Straw Bale Gardening into a small business, Tracey spends much of her time sharing the concept in Australia (and selling BaleGrow as a result). She has especially come to enjoy sharing this great way to garden with kids, who often bring the concept home to their parents. In fact, she has taken her fondness for teaching kids a step further and created BaleGrow Kids, a program designed for kindergarten classes and early-learning programs. With BaleGrow Kids, Tracey teaches young people about gardening sustainably while demonstrating the Straw Bale Gardens method and sharing top picks for growing things at home. BaleGrow Kids introduces many children to gardening and creates an excitement about growing. In fact, there are many studies that prove the efficacy of children's gardening programs in getting kids to eat more fruits and vegetables.

A lovely display Tracey set up at one of the many trade shows where she sells bales and BaleGrow, her bale-prep mixture.

# CONQUERING A WEEDY ALLOTMENT

| NAME | |
|---|---|
| Mark Hill | |
| **LOCATION** | |
| Gravesend, Kent, England | |
| **NUMBER OF BALES** | |
| 12 | |
| **CROPS** | |
| Green beans, herbs, squash, strawberries, tomatoes | |
| **SBG START DATE** | |
| 2015 | |
| **CHALLENGE** | |
| Dealing with bindweed | |
| **FACEBOOK** | |
| Straw Bale Gardening UK | |

IN THE UNITED KINGDOM, as in the United States, community gardening has a long tradition and has grown in popularity as more and more folks seek out the pleasures of growing even when they do not have suitable land for a vegetable garden. Called "allotments" in the United Kingdom, community gardens create an opportunity for scores of gardeners, often allowing people to use a small plot of their own for free or at a very minimal cost. But as anyone who has ever worked a community garden plot can tell you, there are a couple of built-in challenges. One, and it is rare, is the two-legged predators who occasionally help themselves to your prize Mortgage Lifter tomato just when it is at its peak. The other more prevalent problem is weeds. When you garden in an intimate setting with other gardeners, you are at their mercy when it comes to weed control. And it only takes one gardener to lose interest and let a plot full of weeds overrun an entire allotment.

Mark Hill, an allotment gardener in Kent, England, can attest to this. Mark had a running battle with bindweed in his allotment for years and says this was the initial impetus for giving Straw Bale Gardening a go. A passing glance at a post on Facebook that said "no weeding" caught his eye, and his interest was sparked.

His initial research online led him to buy a copy of *Straw Bale Gardens*. The book gave him a quick guide to the new method that he thought could save him from the bindweed backache that he knew was coming his way. Mark says that he understood the concept right away and remarks, "It all sounded quite sensible in theory. I've been accused of being bone idle in the past, so the reduced weeding has made me very keen on the Straw Bale Gardening technique."

As a child growing up in East Sussex (a county in southeast England), Mark spent a lot of time tending the garden with his father. Comprising quite a large area, the soil he tended was likely first cultivated around the fifth century. His father's plot of land was also home to a goat and a few chickens. Even now, Mark recalls the toil of pulling weeds and the resulting backache. Along with asking questions about everything he saw, Mark learned the basics of gardening as every child does—by copying his father's actions around the garden. In Mark's case, he would fall asleep in his own tiny radish plot after growing tired of playing with his toy cars.

When he first broached the idea of Straw Bale Gardening, his fellow gardeners in the allotment were skeptical, and he admittedly was a little nervous about looking the fool. Forging ahead anyway, he had a few setbacks early on. A steady water supply isn't available at his public allotment, but even so, his garden has turned out beautifully and it has done very well with little water.

*Above:* An allotment doesn't provide much space to garden, so planting in bales works out well. Plant more in less space and improve yields.

*Opposite:* Mark posing next to his allotment garden. His smile fairly reflects his opinion of this year's results, including his unexpected success.

I've been told that regular small bales are not available in the United Kingdom. Apparently, those who have given me that worthless information are full of beans!

*Above:* After 12 days of prep, Mark can plant his entire plot in about 2 hours. A pail of water each day keeps the bales moist.

*Opposite:* Mark decided to use netting instead of wires to keep the birds out and to provide support for vine crops.

"Despite my mistakes and best efforts, or rather worst efforts, things still grew in my bales," he says. The skeptics from the springtime even had to admit that his little plot "looked rather fit."

And perhaps most importantly, the bindweed that has plagued his allotment is rendered powerless by the height of the bales and the fact that introducing new "soil" with fresh bales every year or two does not let the weeds get a foothold. Mark also appreciates the plentiful supply of compost the bales generate once they are used up in the garden. Mark enjoys his daily walk to the allotment and the relaxation he experiences from his garden. "I find it encouraging, peaceful, and quiet," he says.

### CROPS

Having little or no previous success with growing peas, Mark was pleasantly surprised by how well they did in bales, as well as by his decreased insect damage. One of his tomatoes has "gone ballistic," says Mark. "It's trying to take over the entire 12-bale patch."

Mark's yearly bindweed backache was almost a memory until his strawberries really took off, and now he must bend quite low to harvest those jewels. "I plan on having more bales next year," says Mark. "I've learned that I like to grow stuff and then eat what I've grown. There is something satisfying about that," he quipped. "I also find being outside in the quiet and open air while caring for the garden relaxing."

### STRAW BALE GARDENING UK

Mark has had some interest in his flourishing bales from friends up at his allotment, and many curious gardeners have asked questions. He started his own Facebook group, Straw Bale Gardening UK, so he can offer advice, discuss the products available in the United Kingdom for conditioning, and address the unique climate in the United Kingdom. Eager to pass along some lessons he has learned, Mark is excited about his future plans. He intends to get his own plot soon, rather than sharing one with his wife, so he can expand.

Mark is a great ambassador for the Straw Bale Gardens method. Now I'm out to convince the rest of the Brits, and that's no small task. Indeed, the British can be a bit skeptical of Yankees when it comes to gardening; after all, they have a 15-century head start.

# PORTRAIT OF A COMMUNITY GARDENER

| NAME |
|---|
| Lynette Perez |
| **LOCATION** |
| Kearny, New Jersey |
| **NUMBER OF BALES** |
| 5 |
| **CROPS** |
| Cucumbers, flowers, peppers, tomatoes |
| **SBG START DATE** |
| 2012 |
| **CHALLENGE** |
| Growing safely in contaminated soil |
| **FACEBOOK** |
| Kearny Community Garden |

A COMMUNITY GARDEN needs many things to succeed: space, access, permissions, articles of charter, garden rules, water, and much more. But most importantly it needs gardeners. The Kearny Community Garden was featured in *Straw Bale Gardens Complete* because it is a great example of how Straw Bale Gardens can make otherwise unusable land suitable for growing wholesome vegetables. In this case, Kearny's ambitious garden gained attention largely because it was created on contaminated land. When traditional flat-earth gardening is thwarted by contaminated soil, Straw Bale Gardening is a viable alternative. Simply cover the soil with a heavy ground cloth and layer on wood chips to keep any roots from penetrating the barrier. With this technique, root systems are entirely safe within the bales, and a 300-bale garden can grow, kept safe from the toxic soil. It's a great story, but it can be a hard sell. "Hey, care to grow some vegetables on this property the EPA has designated as contaminated?"

Well, the good folks who started the Kearny Community Garden in New Jersey know what they are doing, and it is obvious to anyone who walks by. The garden pretty much sells itself. But without the members of the community embracing the garden, none of it would matter. This is the story of one such gardener.

At home in Puerto Rico, Lynette Perez's mother believed in the power of applying cow manure to the garden (similar to my own grandmother in Minnesota). Lynette helped her mother grow beautiful casaba, tomatoes, cucumbers, jalapeños, mangos, sweet potatoes, and beans every year. While Lynette's memories of the days in Puerto Rico are fond, she does recall all the hard work involved in tilling the soil and keeping the garden weeded. Now living in New Jersey, Lynette has become a member of the Kearny Community Garden. After growing vegetables in bales, Lynette is certain she never wants to go back to traditional flat-earth gardening.

Lynette's son heard about Straw Bale Gardens at school one day from a substitute teacher who was going to try to create a Straw Bale Garden in Kearny. Her son told her all about it, and Lynette recalls, "I knew it was going to be absolutely great, and it turns out I was right." Soon after, she signed on.

Lynette's first year growing in straw bales didn't go very well, but it's also accurate to say that growing in bales went much better than she imagined. Starting with just five bales, Lynette bought far too many plants and zealously overplanted each bale. Everything grew like crazy, and Lynette realized that the bales were falling apart from the load of so much plant material.

Spacing plants properly in any garden is important. Remember that the plants will grow, so planting with mature plant size in mind is a great way to master spacing. For many new Straw Bale Gardeners, this can be a difficult lesson. An expert today, Lynette has terrific gardens.

## Joel Says

Straw Bale Gardens are perfect for community gardens because they are low maintenance. Once the conditioning process is completed, the plants just do their thing. Stopping by her garden twice a week to check on things, Lynette goes more often when things are ripening. "It's my hobby—I am committed to it," she says. Lynette especially appreciates being able to garden by sitting on a stool next to her bales—no more kneeling! She deems her garden "therapeutic."

*Above:* Johnny, Lynette's son, uses a wheelbarrow to haul bales on a cold early-spring day. Setup day goes quickly when everyone pitches in.

*Opposite:* It is a busy day early in the season at Kearny Community Garden in Kearny, New Jersey, one of the earliest adopters among community gardens.

Cucumbers, eggplant, and peppers are three of Lynette's favorite crops, and they look almost as great as they taste. Her family loves fresh garden produce.

The Perez family gets 100 percent organically grown produce from their garden, and Lynette loves the idea that she has total control over exactly what she puts into the bales. She uses a natural, organic nitrogen source for the conditioning process and loves the results. Lynette also notices a flavor difference between her vegetables and those grown in traditional flat-earth gardens. Lynette claims, "The peppers definitely have more crunch and flavor. Maybe because they seem to grow faster in the bales than in the soil."

Lynette is an artist, so part of her garden also includes her artwork and creative décor. "I take pride in my garden; I'm an artist, I paint, and I love to decorate my bales, and one year I even built a bridge." Since her husband built a trellis for the bales and a cucumber arch, Lynette enjoys taking pictures of her massive plants from the vantage point of the ground. Lynette says her cucumber trellis looks like a cucumber waterfall when she lies on the ground to take her pictures.

Lynette has shared her love of Straw Bale Gardening with many friends and family members. She has even convinced a coworker and restaurant owner to try this method of gardening. After the latter tasted some of her tomatoes, he plans to serve Straw Bale Garden–grown tomatoes on all his bruschetta at his restaurants next year.

The greatest thing Lynette has done is teaching her kids to garden and encouraging their excitement about gardening. They may not say it out loud today, but someday they will look back and really appreciate the efforts their mother made to grow a garden and teach them how to do it as well. This passion is something that is contagious, and Lynette's excitement about her garden is evident to anyone who has a conversation with her.

### CROPS

Lynette's bales grow a variety of different plants, including cucumbers, peppers, tomatoes, eggplant, and assorted flowers. Lynette likes to change things up every year and visualize what the plants will look like when they are grown. Her family has favorite edibles, so the basics never change: cucumbers, peppers, and especially tomatoes. Lynette does wish she had more bales, but because it is a community garden plot, she has certain space limitations.

### A GARDEN ON A BROWNFIELD?

The Kearny Community Garden happens to be built right on top of what the Environmental Protection Agency refers to as a "brownfield," defined specifically as "a real property, the expansion, redevelopment, or reuse of which may be complicated by the presence or potential presence of a hazardous substance, pollutant, or contaminant." I'm sure your first reaction isn't "Oh yummy, can I eat some of the crops produced in that garden?" But there's more to the story.

Every gardener at Kearny knows Lynette's bales. They're the ones with the colorful décor, wind catchers, and pinwheels—which certainly stand out.

## Joel Says

In traditional flat-earth gardening, packing plants into a garden bed can act as a weed suppressant. When there is literally no room to grow, weeds get crowded out, and the desired vigorous plants are able to grow uninhibited. In Straw Bale Gardens, overplanting isn't necessary to prevent weeds. The growing medium is already free from weed seeds, so there is virtually no weeding with the Straw Bale Gardens method. Even though it's tempting to want to pack many plants into a single straw bale, it's wise to space plants to allow enough room for the size of the plants at maturity. Overplanted and overcrowded bales can fall apart as mature plants literally burst from the bale as they stretch out to gain space.

Several years ago, when looking for a location for a new community garden, the leaders of the movement approached the city government about using this particular plot of ground. After some soil testing, the city essentially refused their request. Due to the obvious risk the contaminated soil posed, it couldn't be used to grow vegetables.

Fortunately, one of the garden organizers encountered the Straw Bale Gardens method and called me for advice. By putting down a layer of thick ground cloth and covering that with wood chips, they could put a bale garden right on top of the contaminated soil, as the roots would never encounter the soil below. It was the ideal solution, and after presenting the Straw Bale Gardens idea, the city approved their request. Seven seasons later, the community garden has become an institution in Kearny, and Lynette Perez and her family are among the many active participants.

# A GARDEN GROWS IN THE BRONX

| | |
|---|---|
| **NAME** | |
| Deborah Roff/Edgewater Park | |
| **LOCATION** | |
| New York City, New York | |
| **NUMBER OF BALES** | |
| 270 | |
| **CROPS** | |
| Beans, cucumbers, eggplant, flowers, peppers, squash, tomatoes | |
| **SBG START DATE** | |
| 2015 | |
| **CHALLENGE** | |
| Salty soil, meeting community needs | |
| **FACEBOOK** | |
| Garden in the Park | |

LIMITED BY POOR, SALTY SOIL, and persistent flooding, a family flower patch nevertheless exhibited the resiliency to succeed over years and generations in a seaside public park called Edgewater Park in the Bronx. Considered one of New York City's "Resiliency Neighborhoods," a community that has experienced or is at risk of flooding, the park is sited along two waterways located near Weir Creek and Eastchester Bay, which sometimes flood the site with the seawater and debris, damaging the soil. Despite the inhospitable conditions, the tenders of the flower patch had a dream of expanding their flower garden into a large community garden where neighbors could stake out a plot.

*Above:* A long-established flower garden was upgraded into a community garden to create the 200-bale Garden in the Park in New York City.

*Opposite:* Garden in the Park, (Edgewater Park, Bronx, New York) has become the talk of the town over the past few years because of its success.

## THE FLOWER GARDEN

After the death of their father, Michael O'Flanagan, Deborah Roff and her sister, Patricia, started a flower garden in an old boatyard at the park. The ground was contaminated, full of salt, rock, and buried garbage, and it had little to no soil. What it did have was all-day sun and a spectacular view of the Long Island Sound. The sisters started to plant flower seeds and were surprised when a few of the flowers actually started growing. Given that the space was periodically inundated with saltwater due to flooding during storms, not everything survived.

A lack of water access on the site also meant that buckets, wagons, and pails were hauled to the site in order to keep the little flower garden growing. Then a friend gave them a cap for a fire hydrant not too far from the garden, which made hauling water easier—but still not easy! The space continued to enchant them, and the sisters kept at it. Friends donated irises, and like the sunflowers the women had planted, they returned every summer. Over time, a few other gardeners joined in to share the dream of a "real garden," helping with the weeding and carrying the water. Deborah says, "When this garden started, it was only a flower garden, and we simply threw little piles of soil on the ground and then planted sunflower seeds. The following year, we were gifted iris and tiger-lily bulbs from gardens belonging to our parents and grandparents. Like old friends, these flowers have returned year after year, despite the flooding from rising tides during hurricanes and storms."

*Top:* While you work, park a chair next to the bales and sit at just the right height to make it comfortable.

*Bottom:* Kids get bored easily these days, but if you keep them busy in the garden and keep their hands full, they won't be able to use their phones.

## GARDEN IN THE PARK

After a decade of tending the garden, Deborah and her gardening neighbors were eager to find a way to establish water access for their small flower plot. They dreamed of expanding and making their garden into a true community garden for Edgewater Park. Although they loved their little flower garden, they wanted to expand the garden to include vegetable plots in a community-garden setting that would bring their neighbors together in a fun and productive experience.

Around that time, Deborah's son gave her a copy of *Straw Bale Gardens*, and she instantly knew: "This method was the answer to our problem."

She and her sister decided to implement the method on their site the following spring. They decided to try a pilot project of 10 straw bales. To isolate the bales from the salty and even toxic soil, they positioned their bales on top of landscape fabric. This provided an inexpensive and viable way to revitalize the space in a vulnerable, flood-prone area. Deborah was confident the bales would eliminate the soil challenges and was curious to see how it would work out. More than bypassing the salt- and garbage-contaminated soil of the site, the Straw Bale Gardens method offered even more benefits to the challenging site: less watering, no weeding, no bending, and amazing food production.

So the sisters posted letters in Edgewater Park, keeping neighbors informed of their straw-bale project. Interest grew, and gardeners gathered, wanting to be a part of it. The response from their neighbors inspired them to create Garden in the Park, a community Straw Bale Garden. Homes are tightly packed together in Edgewater Park, and there is precious little room for gardening. In the face of limited yard space, Garden in the Park solved a need for healthy growing space in the community. Additionally, Hurricane Sandy brought seawater contamination to much of Edgewater Park, so the timing was perfect for a safe and viable community-garden space.

With the organizational help of two friends who were arborists, a plan for a larger Straw Bale Garden the following year was created. But in addition to the plans for Garden in the Park, Deborah and the small group of gardeners needed funds. They applied for a grant from the Citizens Committee for New York funding in 2014, but they did not receive it. They were discouraged but determined to create Garden in the Park in 2015, no matter what.

The second year, the garden expanded to 160 straw bales despite the lack of a grant. The gardeners arranged the bales into 16 plots set up in a rectangular formation. The centers of the bales were filled with organic soil. Deborah and her crew followed the conditioning process and planted crops. Each straw bale cost the gardeners about

$11, making the community garden affordable. At the end of the second growing season, each plot was as unique as the individuals who grew them. After the harvest, the bales were used as compost for the following year's soil.

Garden in the Park has expanded each year since its inception. Currently, there are 270 straw bales, with 25 of the bales dedicated to the Saturday children's program. The youngest members are learning the importance of eating healthy and are becoming little gardeners to be reckoned with. The garden also has 16 bales designated for senior citizens, who receive organic vegetables at no cost from these bales.

It is not just the Edgewater Park community that has embraced Straw Bale Gardening. Two neighboring communities have now adopted and developed their own Straw Bale Gardens, as has a local high school.

### CROPS

In its first season, the garden grew a variety of crops, including cucumbers, tomatoes, butternut squash, eggplant, cabbage, herbs, watermelon, and flowers. Today, each gardener gets to make their own garden plan and plant their bales with any crop they decide to try. This means the plantings are only limited by the assortment of seeds and bedding plants found at the local garden centers. Tomatoes, cucumbers, and peppers are mainstays, of course, but this garden is truly a mix of every variety of vegetable. Flowers and vegetables are organized and interplanted together in some garden plots. The only thing all plots have in common is that they are all planted in bales.

### FINDING A COMMUNITY GARDEN

Deborah Roff is very proud of Garden in the Park but says, "We did not do this alone. Navigating through the process of establishing a community garden led us to Citizens Committee of New York. They offer numerous resources for grassroots projects just like ours, and we are so thankful for the grants they provided."

Many of the expenses for the garden are paid for by the fundraising efforts of the garden members. They share tools, ideas, watering duties, and other work required in the general garden, and members are responsible for maintenance and planting of their own bales. Sharing some of their excess produce with those less fortunate in their own community also helps build a strong sense of camaraderie among members. There is no individual joy that compares to the shared joy you all get from sharing "veggie love bags" with those who don't expect them but truly appreciate the fresh vegetable deliveries.

*Top:* Gardeners are encouraged to decorate their own plots and plant whatever they like. By harvest time, it is an eclectic mix in this garden.

*Bottom:* Check for local resources if you're planning to start a community garden. There are usually grant programs to help cover some startup costs as well.

# A LIVING STUDY IN FRENCH ART

| | |
|---|---|
| **NAME** | |
| Pascale Marq | |
| **LOCATION** | |
| Paris, France | |
| **NUMBER OF BALES** | |
| 300+ | |
| **CROPS** | |
| Beets, grapes, herbs, kale, leeks, peppers, potatoes, squash, tomatoes | |
| **SBG START DATE** | |
| 2013 | |
| **CHALLENGE** | |
| To be voted "Winning Garden Entry" at the 2013 International Festival of Parks and Gardens at Chaumont in the Loire Valley, France | |
| **WEBSITE** | |
| www.pariscotejardin.fr/tag/pascale-marq | |

A FRENCH LANDSCAPE DESIGNER was faced with two challenges on consecutive days: how to obtain high-nutrient vegetables and what kind of garden to enter in a famous French landscape and garden contest. Soon after, Pascale Marq stumbled across Straw Bale Gardens, which proved to be the solution to both challenges.

Pascale's story begins with a visit to her doctor's office. She asked him, "Why am I tired all the time? I eat five servings of fruits and vegetables every day." Her doctor answered, "Yes, madame! But you cannot be certain there are enough vitamins in those fruits and vegetables alone." He went on to explain how most produce is raised in greenhouses, picked early, and shipped (sometimes long distances) to market. Pascale decided that day to try to start her own garden. She knew she could grow better-tasting and healthier vegetables than she was currently feeding her family.

Coincidentally, the next day Pascale received an email regarding the 2013 International Garden Festival at Chaumont-sur-Loire (the Festival International des Jardins Chaumont-sur-Loire). Based in France, the show features over two dozen gardens that are installed for a single growing season to illustrate a design or growing principle. One of the most famous season-long living garden festivals in the world, Chaumont is considered a place to view the best of contemporary trends in gardening. As a practicing landscape designer, Pascale never

*Above:* The International Garden Festival opened in April 2013 and continued into November, with more than 400,000 total visitors walking through this Straw Bale Garden.

*Opposite:* Early in the season after the Straw Bale Garden had been planted on the grounds at Chaumont-sur-Loire castle in the Loire Valley of France.

The heavy timber entry was designed to look like the frame of a beautiful Monet-style French painting of a tranquil countryside in bloom.

misses it. In fact, the festival is a wonderful showcase for garden artists, landscapers, and horticulture professionals, and they submit applications to the festival each year. Out of many hundreds of applications, a jury picks just 25 exhibitors, so being selected is a major honor. The 2013 exhibition was themed "Gardening for the Senses."

Pascale's thoughts about growing better-tasting vegetables felt serendipitous. She started researching online for creative, new, efficient, economical, easy, and productive vegetable gardening techniques. Although Pascale loved the concept of Straw Bale Gardens, she didn't love the look of the gardens. Wanting to enter a Straw Bale Garden in the festival, Pascale set about designing something attention grabbing and attractive.

### A LANDSCAPE TO TASTE

Keeping in mind the rigorous requirements of the application, Pascale began to sketch ideas, all the while trying to make sure the design was educational, enticing, economical, and exciting. Reflecting on the process, Pascale says, "I had to combine a multidisciplinary team composed of landscapers Pierre-Marie Tricaud, a landscape architect at DPLG—former president of the Fédération Française du Paysage—and myself, designer Laurence de Plessix, and landscape-architecture student at ESAJ Emmanuel Taillard. I also received technical help from vegetable-gardening expert Baptiste Pierre from the Vendée region of France and from the extraordinary vegetable-garden experts of la Mothe-Achard in Vendée. We received significant moral support from Mechtild Rössler, director of UNESCO. Finally, but importantly, we

had several sponsors who helped us to create the garden, including the garden magazine *Les Amis du Jardin*, Gabriel d'Orléans Company, and Pépinière Croux."

When the design was finished, Pascale and her team had designed something completely unique, a garden that nobody in the entire world could have ever imagined before, and she planned to build the whole thing out of straw bales. Calling their entry "A Landscape to Taste," the theme was to raise awareness about organic, sustainable food production putting "taste and health on our plates."

After submitting the application, the festival organizers announced Pascale's design had been selected as one of the exhibitions. It was truly the opportunity of a lifetime and the beginning of an extraordinary adventure that would last from January to November of 2013. Planning the garden, Pascale would discover, was the easy part. Building the garden would be incredibly difficult, but her team was up to the challenge.

If you can imagine a painting of an agrarian landscape with rolling hills and fruitful fields, you can envision the look and feel of the exhibit Pascale and her team designed. Cleverly using a heavy timber doorway to frame the entry to the garden, the effect was to echo a framed Monet pastoral painting. The "painting" was composed of four successive hills formed by bales of straw, which were planted with a great diversity of vegetables and plants. Each of these gardens was installed on a space that ranged from 100 to 500 square meters—spaces very compatible with the size of a contemporary town or village garden in France. The bales were installed so those

Illustrations of the garden concept envisioned by Pascale and her team, which changed very little from concept to installation.

In Europe, the soil has been farmed for centuries. So much time can take a toll. Tired soil suffers from depleted nutrients and is made worse with chemical fertilizers and pesticides. The Straw Bale Gardens method allowed Pascale to start fresh and not have to rely on soil. She didn't originally set out to grow in straw bales, but she started doing research and the idea fell into her laptop. She also surmised that she could use the huge volumes of composted straw to rebuild the life and vitality in her original soils. She ultimately wanted to bring the soil back to life, and this seemed like a great way to do it.

nearest the entry were buried completely on one side and then arched up and out, like a gentle hillside. Visitors entered the exhibit through the timber doorway, the frame of the painting, and strolled through the hills in a succession of meals: starter, main dish, dessert, and cheese and wine.

Walking through the painting was designed to be a sensory experience. The walkway inclined slightly around the first hillside and met the second hillside gently rising in the other direction, and the walkways alternated slopes through the third and fourth hillsides. The first hillside was planted with vegetables, herbs, and edible flowers that would be used to make the first course of any civilized French meal, the appetizer or entrée. The second hillside was planted with vegetables and herbs from any typical French main course. Dessert items—berries, edible flowers, herbs, and melon—were on the third hillside. The fourth hillside of the garden was for bread, wine, and cheese and was planted with grapes and included a goat pen in the corner. Humorously, the goat idea didn't really pan out. The goat kept jumping the fence, so she had to go back to her home on the farm.

Because the Straw Bale Garden method was not well known in France, Pascale explained the method, highlighting these key points to visitors:

- In a short period of time conditioning with nitrogen (about 12 days), the bales are ready for planting.

- Without any "tedious work of the soil" and without any input of soil, the plant (as long as it is watered) finds all the necessary elements in this straw, which decomposes slowly.

- This method is ideal for soils that are poor or weakened by years of pesticide treatments.

- After use, the bale serves as compost for other parts of the garden.

Pascale's garden was on display from late April until early November, and I visited in September. Much of the garden had been harvested, but images of the harvested produce were on display in areas where the spent plant stems remained. There were lots of squash, melons, pumpkins, herbs, potatoes, tomatoes, and many other plants still looking splendid. Pascale said, "The visitor went through the garden with the rhythm of the French meal that brings him from the starter to the dessert and all through the seasons from the fields to the final produce harvested, and back to the seeds to start again."

As the visitor reached the back of the garden, the exit was via a long hallway with 7-foot-tall walls of bales and a beautiful display of clear boxes, each filled with seeds of the grains grown in France that could be used to create new bales and vegetables planted in them.

This was very educational and allowed for wonderful traffic flow, with huge numbers of people visiting the garden. An estimated 400,000 to 500,000 visitors walked through the garden that year, and when I met personally with the director of the garden festival, she told me, "In 22 years, we have never had an exhibit that received more interest than the Straw Bale Garden at this year's festival." It was fun to see how much people loved the exhibit.

The Straw Bale Garden agrarian landscape offered a reinvented and enchanting way to grow edibles during the season at Chaumont. The goal of showing visitors a new way to grow better-tasting, natural, healthy, and diverse foods for the table was a success.

The exit hallway was used as a gallery with clear boxes displaying seeds of the common grains and vegetable crops that were grown to create the garden.

### PASCALE MARQ, CERTIFIED SBG INSTRUCTOR

Since the exhibition garden, Pascale has written a lot on the subject and given many conferences in parallel to her work as a landscape designer in France. Pascale specializes in kitchen gardens, town orchards, education gardens for kids, and conservatory gardens. Recently she worked at the castle and garden of Pesselières in Jalognes in France. In fact, her gardens receive quite a bit of media attention.

Pascale has become one of my Certified Straw Bale Gardening Instructors. As a certified Straw Bale Gardening expert, Pascale can share her expertise with folks in France by giving presentations, consulting on a startup projects, or answering questions.

Pascale says, "We are always happy to get letters from people who are thrilled with the Straw Bale Gardens method." She continues to research permaculture techniques and sustainable ways to grow healthy vegetables and fruits. She continues to explain to people how the Straw Bale Gardens method helps eliminate soilborne diseases and insect issues and how it helps rebuild a healthier soil by incorporating large amounts of organic matter into the tired soils, without using manmade fertilizers and pesticides.

# SCHOOLYARD GARDEN

| NAME | |
|---|---|
| Karen Gray/Gideon Pond Elementary | |
| **LOCATION** | |
| Burnsville, Minnesota | |
| **NUMBER OF BALES** | |
| 16 | |
| **CROPS** | |
| Beans, cucumbers, eggplant, peas, peppers, radishes, tomatoes | |
| **SBG START DATE** | |
| 2016 | |
| **CHALLENGE** | |
| Establishing teaching garden at elementary school and obtaining grants to fund the project | |

AT FIRST GLANCE, planting a vegetable garden in a schoolyard sounds like a great idea. And it is. But consistent maintenance is important for most soil-based gardens, and while a garden at a school gets plenty of attention in the early season, it often ends up neglected once the kids are gone for the summer and the hard gardening work begins in earnest. Establishing a schoolyard garden has other challenges too. For one, the soil surrounding schools frequently lacks nutrients and organic compounds, and it can also be costly to do soil improvements and soil-mitigation projects. So, if the soil isn't ideal for gardening, the budget to fix those problems can be prohibitive.

Further, in an existing schoolyard where large trees are already established, it may be difficult to find an ideal location that receives full or near-full sunlight. If large trees have been growing near the area for many years, it is likely the soil in that area is filled with many large tree roots. These roots make tilling the soil difficult, and even if chopped off, they will grow back and steal nutrients and moisture from the garden crops. Finally, the site must also have access to water and be near the school for easy accessibility yet remain out of the way of kids' play zones. The list of challenges is long.

Karen Gray lives not too far from me in Minnesota, where she has been a master gardener for some time. Karen chose to lead an initiative to create a children's garden at Gideon Pond Elementary in the suburb of Burnsville. Locating the garden on the school's property wasn't easy. The group had to consider many issues when selecting a spot, and there were good reasons to dismiss most of the sites. Karen brought to the group the Straw Bale Gardening idea, which she felt would make finding a location much easier. They would still need a sunny location, but tree roots and soil sustainability would no longer be factors. A good fence, a water hose with a hose-end timer, and a pile of weed-free bales of straw would alleviate the other concerns that normally cause challenges for school gardens. At Karen's urging, a plan and proposal for a Straw Bale Garden at the school were assembled.

The first Straw Bale Garden was proposed in late 2015, and a grant from the Jeffers Foundation made it a reality in early 2016. The 10-bale garden was a big success. In 2017, the garden was enlarged to 16 bales and some raised beds were installed, thanks to a grant from the Whole Kids Foundation of Whole Foods Market. With some help from Boy Scouts Pack 435, the garden was set up quickly. A layer of cardboard was first put down to kill the grass underneath, which was be covered with wood mulch once the garden was set up. Several other adult volunteers helped with setting up the fence and some of the heavy lifting involved, but the children were involved in all parts of the setup process. The kids meet at their weekly

*Above:* Excited about learning to garden, the kids would even spend their own recess period in the garden, watering and looking after things.

*Opposite:* Finding the proper location for a garden on a school property isn't easy, especially when large trees with shade and roots need to be avoided.

## Joel Says

My own nephew Noah has always helped his mom (my sister) with her Straw Bale Garden at their home in North Carolina. Noah has autism and has some difficulty focusing—until he finds a subject he likes, and then he really zeroes in on it. When he was nine, he was asked to give a 1-minute speech in class about any subject he'd like. Well, 20 minutes later, his teacher had to ask him to sit down. He had his mom's copy of my first book and was teaching a workshop to the whole room, step-by-step instructions on conditioning bales and all. By the time he was done, many of the other kids' parents were so intrigued that they had to follow up and learn more after the class that day.

*Opposite, top:* Bales are planted with an assortment of vegetables and herbs, some from seed and others transplanted. Labeled plants make it easier to track each crop.

*Opposite, bottom:* Take off three months of summer, put down weed block, install irrigation, use a hose-end timer, and don't forget to harvest!

Project Kids Garden Club to learn about the garden: what makes plants happy, five good bugs and five bad bugs, pollinators, and how to manage pesky rabbits and deer. They all participate in the steps taken to prepare and plant the bales. Watering is also a project that gets spread around to multiple kids. Karen says, "Students often used their recess time to water and tend to the garden."

## AN ONGOING PROGRAM

Norma Hall, a master gardener and teacher, created a curriculum for all three second-grade classes at Gideon Pond Elementary. The students learned about the Straw Bale Gardens process inside the classroom. They also participated in hands-on workshop/garden sessions to work with the bales right outside their back door. The kindergarteners each planted seeds in April to grow indoors and then transplanted those seedlings into the bales in May. Marking their plants for identification allowed them to locate and follow the growth of their plants. It cannot be overstated how much children get out of this experience and how influential a project like this can be on students, teachers, and parents as well.

## CROPS

The garden was planted with many different varieties of crops, including tomatoes, peppers, eggplant, cucumbers, lettuce, radishes, and more. Trellises were installed to support the tomatoes, peas, beans, and cucumbers. The garden was in full glory by late May as the children were leaving school for the summer. Most of them continued to lobby their parents to stop by the school so they could check on the garden over the summer. No weeding and easy watering made summertime care easy for any of the volunteers who committed to keep things going. Harvested produce was donated to local food shelves and benefited many community members with more limited resources who really appreciated the fresh produce.

## LESSONS TO BE LEARNED

Kids absorb lessons that many adults tend to overlook or under-value. Recycling is a great example: the most effective campaign to increase the number of people who were recycling at home was one focused on school kids. They would go home and campaign for their parents to get with the program and separate out the recyclables. They taught mom and dad what they learned at school, and before we knew it, recycling became a habit in many homes all over the country.

Emphasizing the importance of providing habitat for pollinators, school kids are bringing home packets of seeds and passing along the message about protecting bees and butterflies to their parents.

I encourage every vegetable gardener to plant pollinator-friendly flower plots near their vegetable gardens. While bees may seem threatening, the only real threat we all face is the bees disappearing.

The only way the pollen can get from the stamen to the ovum of many of your favorite fruits and vegetables is by riding on the body of an insect. Otherwise, a human being has to use a tiny cotton swab to do it by hand. Imagine if you came home from a long day's work and had to take cotton swabs out to the garden to fertilize flowers for a few hours just to ensure that you had vegetables to eat later that summer. That thought alone should encourage you to pay attention to habitat for pollinator insects.

The list of fruits and vegetables pollinated by bees, butterflies, moths, flies, and beetles is very long. Make sure the pollinators stick around your garden by giving them habitat in your garden and avoiding chemicals that are suspected to be killing bees. While we do not know for absolute certainty what is causing colony-collapse disorder in bees, using neonicotinoids in your garden at this point would be equivalent to tossing a box of aluminum cans and plastic bottles straight into the garbage can: nobody does that anymore.

A schoolyard garden, while it presents challenges, offers more than just fresh produce; it gives kids important life lessons and cultivates a whole new generation of gardeners.

# GROWING A FARM-BASED BUSINESS

| | |
|---|---|
| **NAME** | |
| Jason Ladd/Lucky Ladd Farms | |
| **LOCATION** | |
| Eagleville, Tennessee | |
| **NUMBER OF BALES** | |
| 1,000 | |
| **CROPS** | |
| Cucumbers, eggplant, green beans, okra, peppers, squash, tomatoes | |
| **SBG START DATE** | |
| 2015 | |
| **CHALLENGE** | |
| Carve out a farm-based business in rocky, untillable soil | |
| **WEBSITE** | |
| www.luckyladdfarms.com | |

LUCKY LADD FARMS IS LOCATED on a property not too far from Nashville, on the outskirts of Eagleville, Tennessee. Although the property is labeled a farm, the soil in this specific area has so many rocks that it cannot be tilled or used for growing much of anything. The farm is surrounded by other farms with productive soil, but Lucky Ladd seemed capable of producing nothing but rocks and broken plow blades.

Jason Ladd grew up on a different farm not far from Lucky Ladd. He says, "If you drive a mile or so from the boundaries of my farm here, the soil at many of the farms around mine is fine for growing. I have neighbors growing row crops with good success." Knowing that the rocky soil wouldn't produce much revenue the traditional way, Jason bought the property nonetheless.

Undaunted, he chose to work with what he had and somehow carve a viable farm-based business from the rocky land. He came up with a solution for using the land without having to till the soil and plant crops. And he did it with some unconventional but ambitious ideas.

Initially, Jason opened a family adventure park where kids and adults could come to explore acres of excitement, including over 70 attractions for all ages. Visitors could enjoy farm animals, wagon rides, playgrounds, mega slides, a tractor train, games, mazes, and more. The adventure park is still open spring, summer, and fall, with seasonal entertainment including an Easter-egg hunt, a watermelon festival, a famous corn maze, a pumpkin patch, straw-bale climbing piles, and lots of straw bales everywhere used primarily as décor.

Jason was at a conference in Mississippi a few years back and met another farmer who told him he was growing tomatoes in bales of straw and raved about his success. Jason's first thought was about his rocky soil, and the wheels started turning. He searched online, ordered a copy of *Straw Bale Gardens,* and read it cover to cover. He was convinced. He jumped in with both feet, starting his first Straw Bale Garden with around 700 bales. Pleased with the results, the next year he planted over 900 bales and increased to 1,000 bales the next.

*Opposite:* One thousand bales of straw set up and growing in an area that, soon after harvest, becomes a parking lot for the fall festival crowds.

## Joel Says

One isolated 4-acre plot of tillable land on Jason's farm is able to grow corn each summer. Once the stalks grow 10 to 20 inches high, Jason cuts down selected corn stalks to build a corn maze. He creates a unique design each year and uses a GPS locator to carefully cut out the maze with a lawn mower. The corn maze entertains thousands of kids and adults who try to navigate through it. Recently the corn maze was a very clever Nashville Predators logo in honor of the local professional hockey team.

While it may seem like a lot, a 1,000-bale garden is only 15 rows of 66 bales per double-wide row, plus 10 more used here and there. The garden gets prepared and set with bales once the busy season is over at the farm in the late fall and early winter. The bales are conditioned in the early spring and planted with a whole assortment of vegetable varieties. Drip tape provides the irrigation for the bales, making watering very simple. Once the crops emerge, mature, and ripen, the farm store allows visitors to pick their own vegetables. Jason said, "The popularity of the pick-your-own garden has doubled each year, and people really love it."

He has his own staff follow up to make sure that any crops missed by the picking public are harvested in a timely manner and sold in the farm store as prepicked. He hopes to find a space to leave part of the garden up year-round for the tens of thousands of fall festival visitors they get each year.

At the end of the season, the old bales are knocked over and scattered around on top of the rocky soil of an unpaved parking area using a skid-steer tractor with a spinning brush attachment. There the straw decomposes and quickly becomes soil. Now, after a few years, "The soil is getting quite nice in that parking-lot area,

Once the crops are mature, the garden is opened to the public as a pick-your-own enterprise, with staff finishing the harvest.

and when it rains, we might start to get a muddy mess," Jason said. They may have to start moving the used bales to a new spot where building up new soil would be more helpful.

## CROPS

Other than the corn maze, the rest of Lucky Ladd Farm's crops are in the 1,000-bale pick-your-own garden. It is planted with tomatoes, cucumbers, squash, peppers, eggplant, okra, and lots of green beans. Jason said, "This year we harvested over eighty-five five-gallon pails of green beans, and I don't think anyone on my staff ever wants to see another green bean in their lifetime."

## SPREADING THE MESSAGE

The Straw Bale Garden will likely keep growing at Lucky Ladd as the attraction gains popularity. Jason says people are fascinated with the 10-foot-tall tomato plants he grows, and they love to learn how the Straw Bale Gardening technique works. Jason has even become a "visiting professor" at the local senior center. He says, "They wanted to learn more about the Straw Bale Gardens, so I gave a little talk and invited them all out to see my garden in person."

Over 7,000 children make annual field trips to Lucky Ladd Farms for a day of learning. They have activities and hands-on workshops for the kids. This is truly where Jason's passion comes out. He says, "For many of these kids, this is the first time they have ever seen a farm or pet a farm animal, and most have never seen a cornfield up close or a vegetable garden." Jason's aim is to teach them as much as possible in that 1-day field trip about farm animals, farm crops, and the fun they can have with simple farm activities outdoors. Jason has two very young kids, 4 and 6 years old, and he already has them helping in the garden. He agrees with me that it is very valuable to start teaching young children about growing food. They learn to eat a wider variety of vegetables and sometimes are willing to try new things because they grew them. And once they taste something new, they may turn out to love it.

Jason grew up on a farm. His dad was a gardener, and they always kept a good-size garden for their family. His uncle Donny was a real green-thumb gardener, appearing often in the local paper after growing the biggest watermelon or other gardening achievements. Uncle Donny taught Jason a lot and inspired him to experiment in the garden as well. Jason chuckled a bit when he relayed this story: "The first time my uncle Donny saw me planting in bales of straw, he shook his head and laughed, stating flatly that this would never work." These days, Jason gets a call each fall from Donny requesting 20 bales for his spring gardens. He too has jumped on the bale wagon like so many others. Welcome aboard, Uncle Donny!

Cattle panels arched between rows of bales allow cucumbers and tomatoes to crawl above head height and hang down, tempting passersby. Planting crops for which its easy to determine if they are ripe is key with a pick-your-own garden. Bales love cucumbers, tomatoes, and peppers.

# CHAPTER 5

# SOLUTIONS TO HELP FEED THE WORLD

THE STORIES I'VE HEARD AND OBSERVED from folks outside the United States who have adopted the Straw Bale Gardens method are often the most amazing to me. When I decided to write this book, I wanted to include stories of gardeners who overcame specific and significant challenges by turning to this method. In some cases, this meant overcoming language barriers and adapting the method slightly to fit the situation that exists in these countries. But there isn't any translation required when first-time Straw Bale Gardeners, no matter where they hail from, observe the fantastic results. A huge tomato or pepper plant, or a pail per day of cucumbers, elicits a universal response. The word spreads quickly no matter what language is used to pass along the knowledge. It is amazing to see how many Straw Bale Gardening groups are springing up on Facebook, many of them moderated in foreign languages.

The examples to follow come from an array of climates and a variety of countries covering five continents. On the following pages, you will read about some of the most unique and impressive examples I have found where Straw Bale Gardening has been the solution to a challenging problem. Throughout this book, you will find many stories of Straw Bale Gardens meeting challenges in foreign lands. Those featured in this chapter share one commonality: they are all community programs involving many parties aiming to alleviate hunger.

If you are facing your own gardening challenges and those difficulties have kept you from having the vegetable garden you have always dreamed of, you may find a solution you can use in these profiles. I hope you are as inspired by these folks as I am.

A community-style Straw Bale Garden underway in remote Cambodia.

### From Joel: A Straw Bale Solution to World Hunger

An ancient Buddhist quote says, "There is no sickness like hunger!" Most of us don't really think about that for the most part. I'm guessing that if you could afford to buy this book, you probably have a home or apartment and a place where you can have a garden. It is likely you have already eaten something today, and you'll probably eat again today after you read this. It is painful for most of us to think about people in places on this planet who cannot count on having food to eat today, or any day. How do we solve this problem? What is the solution? What can we do to help?

Some will say that we must donate money or get our government to help these people. We must deliver shiploads of food and thus ensure that these people receive sustenance. Then we go about our lives. The problem, though, is that this doesn't really work very well. The ships do arrive, carrying almost exclusively rice, cornmeal or flour, and beans, which eventually get loaded into trucks. When the trucks arrive in the areas where the starving populations are, the food often ends up under the control of whoever has the biggest guns. Now the guys with guns decide who gets what, and how much. They control the people more easily with this food supply than with the weapons slung over their shoulders. They put a voting ballot in front of a hungry man or woman with hungry kids in tow, and their "democratic vote" continues to perpetuate the same corrupt governments in these "democratic" countries. My wife will attest that if I go more than 8 hours without a sandwich or something to eat, I get darn grumpy, and going a whole day without eating would only ever happen if I had a colonoscopy scheduled the next day. When any person must look to another person for their food supply, it makes them subservient and makes it impossible to stand up against such powers or take control of their own country.

**Straw Bale**
**GARDENS**

Another major concern in many parts of the world today where food aid has become a major source of everyday sustenance is the havoc wreaked on the diets of the population in these regions. The high-carbohydrate diet has spiked the rate of diabetes and has even led to obesity. Yes, the pendulum has swung so far that we now have some places in the world where the hungry poor are now diabetics because of the terrible diet of pure carbohydrates that sustains them.

Why don't they just plant a garden, then, like you do? This is a great solution, I agree, but first they must overcome a few obstacles. They need somewhere to plant, but they own no property and have very little space to live. They have no tools, but working the soil requires at least some basic tools. They need seed, but access to seed is limited. They have little knowledge about gardening, and many in this population are illiterate. They have no fertilizer. They have limited access to water. A garden planted any distance from home could be raided and the produce stolen by other hungry people.

Imagine instead if we delivered just one mechanized baler and one tractor to a rural province in this poor country. The rice farmers who currently burn off their straw because it is considered a waste product are instead paid a small amount to allow us to bale their straw. Making 10,000 bales every week, it wouldn't take long to put a few bales of straw on the front stoops of many of the poorest folks in the area. Delivered with those bales would be a small packet with 20 to 25 seeds and some written and graphic instructions. No tools are required, and human urine works just fine as fertilizer for the conditioning process. Washing and cooking water could be used to water the bales. Soon the population would be eating fresh vegetables they grew at home and learning how to sustain themselves. They could vote for whomever they please and not worry about their children going to bed hungry. There is a solution to world hunger, and it is teaching people how to fish rather than continuing to give them fish. We can help them learn to fish.

"Straw bales" could be hand-formed mounds of rice straw found in Cambodia, mechanically packed rectangles of small-grain straw in the United States, or anything in between. In some cases, straw bales might not be made from straw at all. But whatever the package or type, the Straw Bale Gardening method has been proven to work in all cases, and the world's supply of fresh vegetables is growing.

# THE PIT AND THE PLATEAU: SOLVING THE FLOOD-DROUGHT CYCLE FOR CAMBODIAN FARMERS

| NAME | |
|---|---|
| Nharn Nhov | |
| **LOCATION** | |
| Serei Saophoan, Cambodia | |
| **NUMBER OF FARMS** | |
| 2,700+ | |
| **CROPS** | |
| Beans, bitter melon, cabbage, cucumber, eggplant, leaf lettuce, potato, squash | |
| **SBG START DATE** | |
| 2015, but success came in 2016 | |
| **CHALLENGE** | |
| Flooding, drought, lack of knowledge and resources | |
| **WEBSITE** | |
| www.ockendencambodia.org | |

IN MONSOON CLIMATES, gardening is difficult, to put it mildly. The heavy rains that accompany the monsoons happen to hit right around the time most vegetables are reaching their prime. Flooding drowns plants before they can be harvested. As a result, most of the produce consumed in these countries must be imported, usually at prices typical families cannot afford. And because rice, the one crop that succeeds in these conditions, is a cash crop, most of it is shipped away for export. Hunger is a major issue.

When an enterprising Cambodian government official happened upon some photos of Straw Bale Gardens while doing online research, he had a thought. Countries such as Cambodia might not be rich in fresh produce, but they are rich in straw from the chaff left behind after rice harvest. And like that, a partnership that no one expected was begun. On my end, it started with an email and an offer I eventually could not refuse.

In 2016, I was offered a wonderful opportunity to visit Cambodia and give a special presentation about Straw Bale Gardening to a group of enthusiastic and determined Cambodians from many walks of life: farmers, teachers, government officials, nongovernmental organization (NGO) officials, nonprofit executives, and others. One of the attendees was the official who had happened across the straw-bale images, a gentleman named Nharn Nhov. Nharn is the managing director of Ockenden Cambodia, an NGO aid organization focused on resettlement after mine clearance, training for disaster resilience, developing appropriate technology, and helping provide education for the rural poor. He is doing every day what my grandma would have called "the Lord's work." I liked him immediately, and as I have come to know him, I have seen how effective he is at his job. Quite simply, Nharn does amazing work.

At Nharn's main office in Serei Saophoan, Banteay Meanchey province, he runs a nursery and demonstration garden. He shares his harvest with the staff and shares his knowledge with leading farmers who come to visit from around the province. Farmers from all over rural Cambodia are taught new technology and techniques to help increase their production. They also learn to manage their risk from rain or floods. In 2017 alone, Nharn worked with 2,176 vegetable growers in Cambodia, passing along the information that he learned about Straw Bale Gardening from my presentation.

For Nharn, like many others, the major advantages of this method, such as fewer weeds, fewer insects, and less disease, are major selling points. "Traditional techniques do require a lot of time and hard work," says Nharn. Personally, I must mention much of that work is done in over temperatures 100°F under the hottest sun I've ever experienced.

*Top:* Nharn Nhov (with backpack) shows a visitor around the successful Straw Bale Garden at Ockenden's test plots near their home offices.

*Bottom:* A sign indicates the entry of the demonstration and test garden, where the Ockenden Organization has welcomed thousands of small farmers.

*Opposite:* Many of the farmers and other government officials who came to learn about Straw Bale Gardening were not familiar with straw in bale form.

The demonstration plot at the Ockenden offices has served as an educational and practical garden, teaching and feeding many of the staff members who work there.

## A CHANCE ENCOUNTER: THE RICE-STRAW FESTIVAL

In 2015, Nharn was traveling on the road to Siem Reap province when he saw a whole group of people working in a field and making bales of rice straw. Curious, he stopped and asked questions, finding out that they were working on creating a rice-straw festival. This festival was being organized by KOTRA, the Korea Trade-Investment Promotion Agency's offices in Cambodia, by Mr. Chiho Lee. The purpose of the festival was to celebrate the usefulness of rice straw. During the event, they would emphasize the utility of rice straw for artwork, agritourism, compost, and soil development.

By attracting visitors to their art, entertainment, and food at the festival, they hoped to educate people about the harmful effects of burning straw. Incredibly, most farmers in Cambodia burn the dry rice straw every year to clear it off before they plant a new crop of rice. A major success, the festival drew nearly 40,000 people. It offered huge bale mazes for children to navigate, straw towers for people to climb, singing performances, and large sculptures made from straw. But what would they do with all the bales they made after the festival? That was Nharn's question.

Most Cambodians have never heard of a straw bale. Cambodia is a very warm climate, so bedding material for livestock isn't needed. They do make piles of straw for cows to munch on, but straw, no matter what grain it is derived from, has little nutritional value. Furthermore, cows in Cambodia are free range. After walking around the neighborhood and grazing wherever they like, the cows always come home to the corral at night. Moreover, the farmers do not "feed" them, and they certainly don't provide bedding material. Making a bale of straw was a foreign concept and something new.

## LET THE EXPERIMENTS BEGIN!

After the festival, Nharn ended up with a few bales of straw at his demonstration garden. He'd heard from a friend that you could grow mushrooms on decomposing straw, so he started to experiment. He used some of the bales to make compost for the garden, and used other bales as mulch. And they attempted to grow mushrooms in others, but they were unsuccessful.

In 2016, the rice-festival folks were getting ready to host their event again. This time, they asked Nharn to help. Nharn took 20 rice bales and decided to wet them and put soil on top. Basing his process on the images of Straw Bale Gardening he found online, he planted in the bales and watered the bales the same way he watered his regular garden. Everything quickly died, because unconditioned bales are essentially inert when it comes to nutrition, but Nharn did notice the bales were very hot inside.

A few days later, however, mushrooms of many different types began to grow on top of the bales Nharn had dampened. He searched even more on the Internet, and while he found lots of information, none of it pointed him in quite the right direction. Still, Nharn replanted vegetables in the bales that had sprouted the mushrooms. This time, with the bales now actively decomposing, some vegetables grew, albeit not as well as they did in the soil. Nharn noticed colonies of worms at the bottoms of the bales, though, which he took to be a good sign of an active ecosystem.

Nharn entered some of these bales at the festival and organized them in the manner he saw in the pictures online. Unfortunately, the vegetable growth wasn't as nice as in the pictures online. Nharn understood that he was on to something, but he needed a clearer understanding of the Straw Bale Gardens method.

## BRINGING STRAW BALE GARDENING TO CAMBODIA

Not surprisingly, many farmers were not sure about growing in Straw Bale Gardens, but once they saw the results, at Nharn's bidding, they implemented the techniques on their own farms. Nharn said, "With the support of KOTRA, I expanded the demonstration gardens at the office. Joel Karsten came here to provide the details of his method. Wow! Now the gardens are growing well. We are passing on the information to key farmers and schools all over in Cambodia!"

One of Ockenden's many missions is to help with the mitigation of disasters. For rural Cambodian farmers, disasters usually come in the form of flooding or drought. Introducing new ideas to these rural farmers is not easy; many cannot read and must be taught face to face, one person to another. One by one, the pieces were starting to fit together.

*Top:* I took this picture during a break on one of our classroom lecture days. Communication is difficult when every word requires translation, including questions and answers.

*Bottom:* The national media in Cambodia was very interested in our project, and several articles appeared in Cambodian newspapers featuring both my visit and Straw Bale Gardening.

*Above:* On top of the new plateau, we set up a small demonstration plot for the man and woman pictured here. They served us a wonderful lunch!

*Below:* The pit in the foreground and the mound in the background. An alternative floating garden design is also being tested in the water-filled pit.

## DIGGING A PIT TO STOP A FLOOD

Nharn and the Ockenden organization were in the middle of implementing a new and elegant solution to help many rural Cambodian farmers. They quickly realized how advantageous it could be to integrate the Straw Bale Gardens method into the fix.

The new solution was to dig pits to address flooding. To do this, they use a large backhoe to dig a very large pit in one corner of a Cambodian farmer's farm. Incredibly, this pit is the key to mitigating flooding and drought. The soil excavated from the pit is then piled up and packed down to create a spacious plateau. It is crucial that the plateau be built up well past the high-water flood mark for the area. After the plateau is in place, the pit is left unfilled to serve a new purpose as a reservoir for water that can be scooped out to water crops during a drought. Together, the pit and the plateau are an ingenious solution for an age-old problem in Cambodia.

The top of the plateau is made from zero-organic-matter soil dug up from the bottom of the pit that is useless for growing crops. This is where Straw Bale Gardening enters the picture. Simply placing a few dozen rice straw bales on top of the plateau turns the space into a productive garden. Because the plateau is above the highest flood line, there is no chance of flooding in the garden. Talk about being high and dry! Any additional rainwater or runoff left behind in the pit simply contributes to the reservoir. While not potable (meaning the water cannot be used for drinking), the

greywater in the reservoir is ideal for watering the bales or other crops when drought arrives.

Now, digging a pit certainly isn't rocket science, but this solution absolutely works. As Nharn can attest, the pit-and-plateau technique is helping mitigate the flood and drought risk for these small-scale farmers. Once decomposed, the bales on the plateau leave behind a layer of beautiful compost. In a few years, that compost will suffice as a growing medium for other crops that take up too much space to be planted in bales.

Meeting and working with Nharn was a thrill for me, but he is the one truly in the trenches (or the pit, as it were). In a part of the world where hunger is still an issue and where a flood or drought can mean starvation for a family or a whole province, teaching farmers how to be more successful growers is paramount.

You can find more about Nharn on his website at www.ockenden cambodia.org.

A handmade wood baler is used to compress loose rice straw into tight bales. The compression is key to rapid decomposition.

# NO SPACE, NO TOOLS, NO EXCUSES

| | |
|---|---|
| **NAME** | |
| Jonavie Paclibar | |
| **LOCATION** | |
| Davao, Philippines | |
| **NUMBER OF BALES** | |
| Hundreds | |
| **CROPS** | |
| Gourds, lettuce | |
| **SBG START DATE** | |
| 2017 | |
| **CHALLENGE** | |
| Lack of property or tools for growing produce | |
| **FACEBOOK** | |
| Philippines Rice Straw Bale Gardening | |

EVEN IN WEALTHY NATIONS with sophisticated urban cores, the idea of growing a lush vegetable garden seems like something of a nonstarter. You might nurture a container of cherry tomatoes and a few herbs, but most urban dwellers don't think beyond that. The lack of space and resources is even more of an issue in some less prosperous nations, where growing your own produce feels like an impossible dream. But whether you live in New York or Manila, you can grow your own crops, and all it takes is some optimism and some straw.

Jonavie Paclibar is a young woman from the Davao area of the Philippines. In the fall of 2016, Jonavie sent me an email asking for more information on the Straw Bale Gardening technique she had read about on my website and Facebook page. Jonavie was optimistic that this method might work to solve some problems for vegetable gardening in her country. Unlike many in her country, Jonavie was extremely knowledgeable about horticulture. In fact, Jonavie is very young (only five years out of high school), so I wondered how she could have such knowledge and interest in advanced agricultural studies. I soon discovered that this young woman was quite intelligent and learned quickly.

We began to exchange emails, in which she answered many of my questions about her specific knowledge of fungal and bacterial reproduction. Additionally, Jonavie helped me research how specific strains interacted with and encouraged the breakdown of rice straw, which is prevalent in the Philippines. All the while, Jonavie was learning more about the specifics of the Straw Bale Gardens method. We had many lively back-and-forth emails in which we both learned from each other.

Jonavie's personal story is inspiring. She is the oldest of five children. Her mother passed away when she was only 14, so out of necessity, Jonavie stepped into the matriarch role for her family at that very young age. Growing up on a rice farm outside of Davao, her family had been involved in agriculture for many generations.

After graduating from high school, Jonavie received a 2-year technical-college certificate. She landed a job as a lab technologist managing a rather large staff for a tissue-culture lab in Davao. On the home front, Jonavie was caring for her father, her siblings, and a newborn baby all alone after her fiancé got cold feet. With all this going on, she was very motivated to find a way to grow food at home without using soil. Like most people in her country, Jonavie didn't have a place to grow near her rented home in the city.

Knowing the limitations faced by for her fellow Filipinos, Jonavie believes the Straw Bale Garden method is a viable solution for vast urban populations in the Philippines. The method offers some distinct advantages: it allows people to easily learn to grow a few vegetables in a few bales of straw without needing tools, and you also don't

*Opposite:* Here, students learn ways to use rice straw bales to overcome many of the climate and soil issues they encounter in the Philippines. The University of Southeastern Philippines, and ACES Polytechnic, each set up demonstration gardens for students.

have to spend any money to buy fertilizers or supplies. During a time when her own future was extremely pressured and uncertain, Jonavie's concern for her fellow citizens really told me a great deal about this young woman.

### SHARING THE METHOD

After Jonavie planted a garden at her own home, she could hardly contain her enthusiasm for Straw Bale Gardening. In her excitement, she contacted both the University of Southeastern Philippines (her alma mater) and the ACES Polytechnic College to see if they would be interested in testing this new method of growing. Eager to share in the success, Jonavie helped both schools set up large demonstration gardens. She then began teaching the students and professors at these two influential educational institutions about the specifics of the method.

Jonavie tended her own garden as well as her two project gardens in addition to taking care of a newborn baby, four siblings, and a father with many health problems. Despite her many obligations, Jonavie still managed to smile in most of the pictures she sent back to me.

We learned quickly that in the Philippines' tropical climate, handmade rice-straw bales decompose rapidly. A planting bed with split bamboo works well.

## DEMONSTRATING SUCCESS

The demonstration gardens grew very well. As Jonavie sent nearly daily reports, the lessons learned were many. The tropical climate with high temperatures and heavy rains caused the bales to decompose more rapidly in the Philippines than in our climates in the United States. Being handmade, the bales were not very tightly compressed, which also may have contributed to the rapid decomposition.

Today, new projects with bigger and tighter bales are already underway. Targeting the urban poor populations, Jonavie is helping people find and purchase bales at a low cost so that they can start their own city Straw Bale Gardens. Tirelessly traveling throughout her home province and more remote areas of the Philippines, these days Jonavie leads workshops to teach Straw Bale Gardening to many curious people. By the end of the workshop, participants have prepared one- to three-bale gardens on a front patio, rooftop, or any space where the sun shines. By prepping the bales with urine (high in nitrogen) and greywater, Filipinos can achieve the same results required for Straw Bale Gardening anywhere: conditioned bales.

It is quite something to witness the transformation that takes place when disadvantaged people who never dreamed they could grow their own food discover that it is possible. In fact, it is fairly easy, even in these conditions, to provide fresh, healthy food for their family. Growing vegetables in straw is a practical and productive solution for Filipinos too. It costs them almost nothing to grow lots of healthy, organic food for themselves and their families.

*Left:* Rice straw is a plentiful waste product that farmers normally burn off the fields before replanting. Not anymore; now it can be baled and sold.

*Right:* Lettuce crops were ready to harvest within 30 to 40 days. Bales allow drainage; even heavy rainfall doesn't cause the normal problems as with soil.

## Joel Says

Greywater is water left over from bathing and dishwashing. In developed countries, this water is often poured down the drain. However, folks in drought-stricken areas like California recognize the value of greywater; it also contains natural fertilizers and nutrients.

*Left:* A student watering the bales in the test plot. Most students had never seen a bale of straw when the project began.

*Right:* The participants selected the vegetable crops they would plant and included bitter gourd, which is popular there but was something new to me.

## THE SETUP: UNIVERSITIES

The demonstration gardens at the University of Southeast Philippines (USeP) and ACES were set up in long end-to-end rows with a trellis system over the tops of bales planted with vining crops. The bales were conditioned in two ways: with a typical urea nitrogen fertilizer at USeP and with an organic nitrogen fertilizer at ACES. Within 6 or 7 days of beginning the conditioning process, both projects yielded wild mushroom growth. While the bales showed good signs of breaking down quickly and were planted or seeded earlier than I normally recommend, they achieved excellent results. As the project manager, Jonavie collected data about production and made many notes about her observations. Jonavie personally photographed the gardens, and her photos are the ones you see in this book.

## THE SETUP: URBAN HOME GARDENS

The small urban home gardens consist mainly of one, two, or three bales. Investing only their time, most of the participants have spent no money on their Straw Bale Gardens. Provided with instructions for preparation and planting, including information on how to water and deal with insects or other pest problems using simple organic solutions, the participants often know next to nothing about gardening at the beginning of the project. With a short, 90-day garden production-and-harvest cycle for most crops, the first-time gardeners learn a great deal about growing their own food.

## LOOKING TO THE FUTURE

I am excited about the future of Straw Bale Gardening in the Philippines, and I think it could change much of the thought process that government officials have when it comes to finding solutions for hunger in urban populations. Like other projects I have been involved with, the Philippines project started very small, but the excitement from the participants who have a chance to see the results is encouraging. Like many avid Straw Bale Gardeners, Jonavie set up a Facebook page specifically for Filipino Straw Bale Gardeners. In less than 5 months, Jonavie had over 14,000 members follow her page. As a Certified Straw Bale Gardening Instructor, Jonavie is now offering workshops and providing leadership on this method throughout the Philippines.

## CROPS

The main crops tested in the Filipino bales included several that were selected because they are popular vegetables in the diet of a typical resident of the region. For instance, bitter gourds, lettuce, cucumbers, and other leafy greens were planted and yielded great success in the bales. Most produce was mature in fewer than 60 days, and the leafy greens produced two crops in the same 60-day period. The handmade bales for the demonstration gardens were made too small and were not compacted enough to last much beyond 90 days; they collapsed and decomposed entirely during that short time in the hot, humid climate of the Philippines.

### Joel Says

In the Philippines, the average urbanite rents the property where they live and has very limited space. Taken for granted in developed countries, community gardens do not exist in the Philippines. Why? Mainly because a community garden would be planted by some and harvested by many, including folks who are hungry but didn't participate until harvest time. To many Filipinos, a community garden is unsustainable.

Rory Pepito Roque, a farmer who lives near Davao, set up a Straw Bale Garden. He's having such great success that he is already expanding.

Growing vegetables doesn't require a big investment. With inexpensive, handmade rice-straw bales, all it takes is a small space with full sun and seeds.

## GROWING TO EXTREMES

The Philippines has many extreme growing challenges. Close to the equator, it has essentially two seasons: the wet season and the dry season. Both extreme seasons can be difficult for growing vegetables that thrive in consistently moist and well-drained media. Beginning in June, the monsoon seasons brings many days of torrential rainfall followed by hot sunshine. Come October, the dry season makes rain a rare event. Many crops require irrigation to produce any yield.

Using traditional methods, crops certainly can grow year-round in the Philippines—provided growers use properly built raised beds and soil modifications. Tenting their small gardens from the monsoons and shading them from the heat of the dry-season sun are done in some very creative ways and can improve production. While it is possible to make raised beds and modify the soil to create the necessary drainage that will allow crops to survive the monsoon rains, that solution poses a problem during the dry season, when good drainage leads to parched, stressed, and struggling beds.

This is where Straw Bale Gardening offers a unique solution and truly shines. When they are fresh, the bales excel at shedding excess water. Once the bales begin to break down, however, they hold moisture well. This dual functionality is perfect for the weather extremes in the Philippines. When the monsoon season starts, the new bales will release excess water. As the dry season arrives, the bales will serve nicely as a reservoir of moisture for crops that need it. In a nutshell, the bales are ideal for these climate extremes. If made big enough and densely compacted, the bales will survive for a full year, producing several crops. Afterward, the bales continue to give as they serve as rich compost. Straw-bale compost can be used to modify heavy soils with fine clay texture and improve the existing soil's production capacity as well.

## THE UNIVERSAL FERTILIZER

Filipinos without access to purchased fertilizer products have learned that they can prepare or condition their bales using a simple and readily available organic nitrogen source. It is one that all mammals, including humans, manufacture themselves a few times each day: urine. Bale conditioning can be accomplished by collecting and applying 3 or 4 gallons of urine, human or otherwise, to each bale over a period of 10 days. Human urine has a 10 to 12 percent nitrogen content. Though much of the nitrogen from urine is volatilized and lost in the form of ammonia gas, enough nitrogen remains to encourage and feed the growth of bacteria for conditioning the bales. While we Westerners tend to be put off by the idea of using urine as a fertilizer, it contains enough nitrogen to do the conditioning job very well. The plants will grow for a month or two, during which no more urine will be added, and the plants harvested will be completely urine free.

## SOURCING STRAW AND MAKING BALES

For urban dwellers, regardless of which country they hail from, locating bales of straw can be the most difficult part of the process. But it is especially difficult in locales such as the Philippines, where bales must be fashioned by hand. Unfortunately, Filipino farmers have little understanding of the value of the rice straw that remains after their harvest. As a result, most rice farmers in the Philippines simply burn off the straw when it dries to prepare for the next planting season. Once introduced to the notion that bales made from their straw can be sold profitably, however, the rice farmers will surely stop burning their straw in favor of baling it.

In order to make bales, Filipinos typically follow plans found online on how to fashion a simple wood hand baler. Urban gardeners are able to purchase the bales at a very low cost. In these rural areas, most bales are available for less than 50 cents each. Should the method really take off and grow (I think it will), I anticipate a few square balers could be imported and used to generate thousands of bales for urban populations all over the Philippines.

*Top:* Peppers are a universal crop, recognized around the world and used in every cuisine on earth, from the Philippines to Philadelphia. Peppers love bales.

*Middle:* Locate a few bales wherever the sun shines and they are handy. Prepare them with yellow liquid fertilizer, collected from the family for 2 weeks, then plant.

*Bottom:* Rory Pepito Roque has expanded the Straw Bale Garden at his farm and is leading the way in demonstrating the method for many of his neighbors.

# FLASH GARDEN FOR DEPLETED SOIL

| | |
|---|---|
| **NAME** | |
| Paul van Hedel | |
| **LOCATION** | |
| Eindhoven, Netherlands | |
| **NUMBER OF BALES** | |
| Hundreds | |
| **CROPS** | |
| Mushrooms, peppers, squash, tomatoes, and more | |
| **SBG START DATE** | |
| 2012 | |
| **CHALLENGE** | |
| Depleted soil from mono-cropping, making it difficult to grow sustainable edibles, especially in urban areas | |
| **WEBSITE** | |
| www.5dsolutions.nl | |

AS YOU HAVE SEEN AND WILL SEE throughout this book, Straw Bale Gardening can be the solution to many garden challenges. Across the planet, more and more folks are adopting the method and using it to growing vegetables where they would not grow before. This gratifies and humbles me. I have met many of these innovators and been astonished by how they have made the method their own and adapted it to their particular situation. But few Straw Bale Gardeners have made an impression on me like Paul van Handel. For Paul, it is not enough just to grow a functional and productive urban Straw Bale Garden—for him, you have to do it with some serious fun, a dose of art, and some rock-and-roll attitude.

Yes, Paul is quite a character. By the time he was 12, he handed his parents a fully detailed, drawn-to-perfection garden design for their property. He even included a materials list. With the mind of an engineer and the heart of a philanthropist, Paul uses his passion for horticulture to help others. Paul's gardens are designed to inspire, educate, and produce food for the public without creating waste or requiring any unsustainable inputs.

In 2011, Paul attended a permaculture design course, which was "an eye opener" for him. Looking for a system that would better emulate the natural world, Paul recognized the potential for urban areas after watching an online video I produced about the Straw Bale Gardens method. Paul recalls, "I saw Straw Bale Gardens as a perfect way to grow food, create no waste, have a balanced ecosystem, at a low cost and with little effort to obtain great yields." Paul strives to follow basic permaculture principals, such as energy storage and producing sustainable food, using all 12 ethical design rules (as outlined by David Holmgren in his book *Permaculture: Principles and Pathways Beyond Sustainability*) that define a nondisruptive edible landscape.

Thrilled with the Straw Bale Gardens method, Paul set out to create greater public awareness of the benefits of growing in straw bales. Not a fan of following bureaucratic rules, Paul has a daring and unique approach to creating public garden spaces.

Acquiring almost every input for his gardens for free or at very low cost, Paul spends "nearly nothing" on the materials he uses to create his gardens. The trellises, signage, fencing, and artistic elements are all scavenged or made from waste building materials. When free bales cannot be sourced, Paul will pay small fees for bales from farmers. However, most of the time, Paul finds donations of unusable (wet) animal bedding material for no cost.

A developer of very innovative gardening technology and products, Paul works with surrounding living fences, window farming, aquaponics, and hydroponics in the Netherlands.

For several years, Paul battled chronic fatigue syndrome. Given his activities today, it is hard to imagine Paul without his trademark energy. However, switching to an entirely raw-food diet allowed Paul

*Opposite:* One of Paul's earliest projects was designed to fit a specific urban space, to educate and intrigue passersby, and to be low maintenance. Mission accomplished.

*Top:* While every garden must grow crops, of course, the best gardens happen when they include creativity and an artistic urban touch in the overall design.

*Bottom:* Paul rarely pays money for any of the materials he uses in the gardens he builds. Instead, he repurposes discarded materials and gets great results.

to overcome his illness. Paul claims, "Eating only raw food completely changed my energy level, and it has increased my creativity. I spend more time learning, and I feel encouraged to try new ideas."

## FLASH GARDENS

If you're familiar with the term "flash mob," then you'll get the gist of what I mean when I say "flash garden." Incredibly, Paul has created many flash gardens of different shapes and sizes and in various public locations around his city in the North Brabant region of the Netherlands. This past spring, Paul created what he called "a food-maze garden in carefully selected public space."

I think it may be best not to dig too deeply into whether Paul actually receives permission to use the public spaces for the flash gardens he has created in and around Eindhoven. Although Paul is vague about who owns the actual spaces where many of his Straw Bale Gardens have popped up, they are always very public places. As Paul says, "Once the garden is set up and it looks nice, it's interesting. When people see the garden growing and producing food, they like it. The gardens have never been vandalized or removed."

After the flash garden is installed, Paul puts up signs that encourage people to harvest anything they desire so it doesn't go to waste. The public is also free to plant additional seeds of anything they would like to grow if they can find unused space in the bales.

Paul's involvement in Straw Bale Gardening is not limited to the streets. He shares a mission to draw new Straw Bale Gardeners in. Now an experienced Straw Bale Gardener himself, Paul offers seminars to teach people the technique. Paul says, "I intend to educate an army of Straw Bale Gardeners and put gardens all over inside the city in wasteful public spaces. In turn, these 'city farmers' can pay for themselves by selling some of the extra organic produce to restaurants. The participants can also give workshops, and maybe give any excess vegetables to food programs for the poor."

Ingeniously, most of Paul's gardens are set up with automated irrigation and moisture sensors, using a system that is quite advanced. Even more fantastic is the fact that Paul runs all his irrigation systems with his iPhone. "My goal is to make these gardens completely maintenance free so they require nothing after planting until they begin producing."

Paul's affinity for using straw bales to build gardens has become quite well known in Eindhoven. His installations have drawn public attention and are proving that unused urban spaces can be easily converted into productive community-garden spaces, producing significant amounts of fruits and vegetables with little effort.

## CROPS

Paul plants a variety of plants in his pop-up gardens, including tomatoes, peppers, strawberries, oyster mushrooms, pumpkins, and summer squash. After he starts his crops, Paul encourages the public to plant whatever they like, leaving some of the bale surface coated with a prepared seedbed that's ready to plant. Later, Paul mulches the tops of all the bales with a thick layer of sawdust. This is a trick Paul came up with on his own, and he claims it helps hold in moisture and prevents insect damage. I can't comment on the efficacy of doing this—I've never mulched with sawdust. Rest assured, if Paul does it, there must be something to it. I might try it next year on a few bales myself.

*Top:* This simple sketch layout for a unique Straw Bale Garden maze became Paul's latest creation and another urban-garden calling card.

*Bottom:* The maze garden came to life in 2017 and became one of Paul's best signature gardens. The irrigation is completely controlled by an app on his phone.

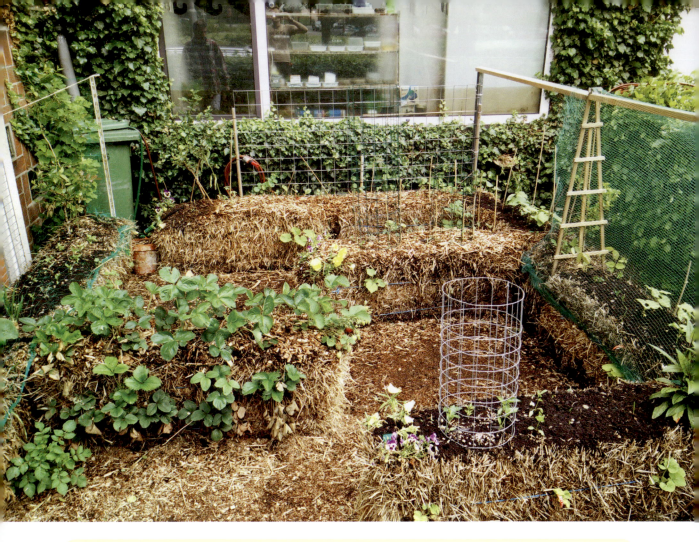

## Joel Says

In my mind, the word *sustainable* has a specific connotation when it comes to agriculture, horticulture, and food production. To me, sustainability used to mean implementing techniques that would likely cause a reduction of productivity, requiring extreme inputs of labor to keep the system "sustainable." I saw sustainability as a linear process—with a distinct start and a definite endpoint. At least, this is what I thought prior to meeting Paul.

Paul presents an alternative perspective on the topic of sustainability and Straw Bale Gardens. Paul does not see sustainability as linear. To Paul, sustainability is an infinite loop. The continuous "sustainable" looping system of bale gardening results in growing a high-production capacity with ultra-low labor inputs. Paul glowingly points out that Straw Bale Gardening meets all 12 of the ethical principles of a "sustainable edible landscape system." When asked to illustrate sustainability in Straw Bale Gardening, Paul draws an elegant cycle of life, growth, and decomposition—an infinite, completely closed-loop production system requiring only waste inputs, sunshine, and limited water.

*Above:* One benefit of using the Straw Bale Garden method is that every year you have an opportunity to rearrange the bales into something new.

*Right:* A garden planted in vertically stacked bales along a wall in an out-of-the-way urban location. A signature van Hedel "flash garden."

*Opposite:* In less than 100 square feet, this 10-bale garden produced a selection of vegetables for an entire family, and did it while looking tidy on concrete.

# THE MOLLY BLACKBURN STRAW BALE GARDEN

| NAME | |
|---|---|
| Ben Tiervlei | |
| **LOCATION** | |
| Molly Blackburn, South Africa | |
| **NUMBER OF BALES** | |
| 80 | |
| **CROPS** | |
| Beans, peppers, squash, tomatoes | |
| **SBG START DATE** | |
| 2017 | |
| **CHALLENGE** | |
| Compact, heavy clay soil devoid of nutrients, extreme poverty | |
| **WEBSITE** | |
| www.universalpromise.org | |

COMPACTED, ALKALINE, HEAVY CLAY SOILS are the norm in and around Molly Blackburn, an informal settlement literally built on a former dumping grounds in the Eastern Cape of South Africa. The reason most consider this land worthless and unproductive is likely also the reason it has become the home of some of the poorest people of South Africa. The soil is almost nonexistent here, and certainly not alive. The lack of electricity, clean water, and proper housing, not to mention gardening tools, is a challenge to any person who might exert the effort to plant a traditional garden.

Plants aside, sometimes even human beings find it a challenge to stay alive in Molly Blackburn. With makeshift shacks for housing, rampant disease, unemployment, and low wages, even the most willing have an almost impossible task in tackling the difficult physical labor of working up the soil for a garden. The basic knowledge needed for growing a vegetable garden is simply out of reach for most people in this part of the world. Should anyone establish a successful garden plot anywhere other than immediately adjacent to where they live, the poverty-stricken population would likely help themselves to the harvest, and all the work would be for nothing. Because inexpensive food is often unhealthy and high in carbohydrates, such as cornmeal, rice, and beans, the diets of these poor populations have led to an explosion in diseases such as diabetes and have even caused obesity among many of the poor.

When Universal Promise, a US-based 501(c)(3) nonprofit, arranged to bring in 80 bales of straw for a large demonstration garden project, they looked immediately to Ben Tiervlei as a community leader to manage the project for them. Lining up a row of heavy bales might seem like a lot of work to some of us, but for Ben, a 35-year-old Molly Blackburn resident, it was a pretty easy task. The idea was to put bales within a few feet of the residences of a whole group of people willing to participate in the effort. Ben would teach them, hands on and step by step, the entire process. Bypassing the soil and growing directly in the bales, the Molly Blackburn Straw Bale Garden eliminated concerns over the contamination in the existing soil. After 15 years of composting and creating his own soil, Ben had already built up a vegetable garden at his home in Molly Blackburn. His well-established interest in gardening made Ben a natural fit to transfer his skills to the new Straw Bale Gardens method. His objective now is to teach the rest of Molly Blackburn the basics of Straw Bale Gardening.

After agreeing to work on the project, Ben suffered a personal loss when his fiancée died due to illness. Through it all, Ben has forged ahead with the project. He is an endearing character who has a vibrant sense of humor and a command of three languages. Ben was born in the Eastern Cape, and his parents both passed away

*Opposite, top left:* Ben and another volunteer carry a bale from the delivery truck. The excitement of a new project is reflected in his smile.

*Top right:* Carrying a bale on her head, this woman is one of the volunteer gardening participants in the Straw Bale Gardening project in Molly Blackburn.

*Bottom left:* The whole town seemed to turn out for the first day of the Straw Bale Gardening project. There were plenty of volunteers to help unload bales.

*Bottom right:* People use buckets to moisten bales with water after the first application of fertilizer. Nothing is easy in Molly Blackburn—no garden hoses or spigots.

One of the volunteers holding up a copy of *Straw Bale Gardens Complete*, the guide they are relying on for guidance on their new project.

when he was quite young, forcing him to fend for himself. He found himself in Molly Blackburn 15 years ago, and now he's invested in making it a better place. Ben has dreams beyond his garden fence of becoming a radio personality, talk-show host, or tour guide. For now, he is focusing on his Straw Bale Gardening project and mourning the loss of his fiancée.

The ultimate goal of this project is to fuel the number-one mission of Universal Promise: education for all. It was instantly clear, however, when Universal Promise first found Molly Blackburn that the lack of financial empowerment and proper healthcare were at the root of many problems.

Combating disease is inextricably linked to proper nutrition, so with that in mind, Universal Promise launched the Straw Bale Gardening project. Growing healthy food is the first step to getting healthy and then getting a proper education.

Ben is great at motivating people, and he likes to write stories about others. He survives and thrives in Molly Blackburn through his determination, intelligence, charisma, and eagerness to learn. That eagerness prompted Ben—both as a form of self-protection and to avoid the hunger that plagues his community—to study and master gardening. He is now sharing that craft and his leadership to benefit his neighbors and friends who are participants in the Straw Bale Gardening pilot project.

### PROJECT DETAILS

A variety of participants who showed interest early on in the project were selected to receive bales, which were then delivered to their homes. Hands-on demonstrations were offered to each participant. With a population of about 2,500 and approximately 500 households, it is likely that everyone in Molly Blackburn knows someone who is part of the Straw Bale Garden project. Ben says his goal is "to bring a Straw Bale Garden to as many homes as are interested." If 100 percent were eventually recruited to participate, it is believed that Straw Bale Gardening could have a dramatically positive impact on hunger, diabetes, cholesterol, blood pressure, maternal and infant healthcare, hopelessness, and much more.

Residents made a good turnout for the introductory session. Attendees were in high spirits and were receptive to the follow-along visits made by Ben and other volunteers over the 12 days of the conditioning period. Some participants needed reminders about where to place the bales and the extent to which they should be watering. They were all open to learning and happily adjusted.

Participants were thrilled by how quickly their efforts began to pay off. They did not have to wait weeks and weeks to see the impact. After a handful of days into the process, they began to see sprouts.

*Top:* Bales were readily available from local farmers in this part of South Africa, though I was surprised by how expensive they were, at $6 each.

*Bottom:* Martha Cummings, the founder and executive director of Universal Promise, demonstrates how much fertilizer to use on each bale.

## CROPS

The main crops for the pilot project were tomatoes, beans, squash, peppers, potatoes, and cabbage. The selection of crops being grown was a bit limited due to availability. Plans going forward include introducing a variety of new vegetable options. Ben will be teaching others how to collect, dry, and save seeds for replanting the next season, as he already does in his own vegetable garden. Hybrid seed isn't nearly as plentiful in this part of the world, and using them may be something that Universal Promise, and their benefactors, can help with in the future. Seeds are small, and a lot of vegetables seeds can fit into one suitcase.

## UNIVERSAL PROMISE

We have all heard the heartbreaking stories about starving children, and we've watched the television commercials bringing the plight of the people in these disadvantaged countries to our attention and asking for our support. Imagine if your support could buy a bale of straw, and if that single bale of straw served as an inspiration to a family to plant an entire garden that produced enough food to feed their whole family. The fresh vegetables would change their diet and improve their health. Their healthy children would able to attend school and receive an education, changing the course of an entire family. Send a bag of cornmeal to a family and you might feed them for a day, but if you send a straw bale to the same family, you may help them learn to feed themselves for a lifetime. Get in touch with Universal Promise at www.universalpromise.org or find them on Facebook.

The youngest participant, helping water. Teach a child to grow food and you forever stack the deck so it's likely they will never go hungry.

# MADE IN THE SHADE WITH DIY BALES

| | |
|---|---|
| **NAME** | |
| Wesley Currin, a.k.a. Bozz Man | |
| **LOCATION** | |
| Lichtenburg, North West, South Africa | |
| **NUMBER OF BALES** | |
| 150+ | |
| **CROPS** | |
| Barley, basil, beans, carrots, chili peppers, eggplant, parsley, tomatoes, wheat, zucchini | |
| **SBG START DATE** | |
| 2015 | |
| **CHALLENGE** | |
| Heat, existing heavy unproductive soils, drought | |
| **FACEBOOK** | |
| BOZZ MAN | |

A NATURALLY HOT CLIMATE coupled with an unusually protracted drought will challenge any gardener. Sometimes the best answer to a confounding problem is simple creativity and a willingness to try something new. And in the case of gardening, boundless enthusiasm and curiosity for the subject help too.

Although Wesley Currin's background is in IT and research, he has always had a keen interest in plants and trees. Spending time as a child in his father's greenhouse and garden, Wesley developed a strong interest in permaculture and organic farming methods. A true plant addict, Wesley grows bonsai pots, cacti, herbs, succulents, and vegetables on his own farm in the North West province of South Africa. Always curious to learn about new methods of growing, Wesley has been experimenting with aeroponics, aquaponics, and hydroponics. He also has a growing interest in Korean natural farming and probiotic farming practices. As a trained researcher, Wesley doesn't leave many stones unturned when he gets interested in a topic.

Wesley's interest in growing in bales started accidentally after he discovered composting. As an avid composter, Wesley created several large heaps on his farm. His composting efforts created many opportunities to learn about decomposition and the amazing biological activity that takes place when materials begin to break down.

When a neighbor offered him a huge pile of moldy round hay bales, Wesley ripped them apart. He made his own bales by packing the hay into a 40-gallon container and stomping it down. He added water to saturate the hay and used a big rock to keep the hay submerged for an entire hour before he dumped out the newly formed and fully saturated bale. Excited to carry the process forward, Wesley added organic nitrogen fertilizer in the form of liquid manure, compost tea, and fermented plant juice before finally adding a thin layer of soil over the surface of the bales. A couple of weeks later, the bales began to sprout mushrooms. Next, the seeds and transplants quickly shot up out of the bales. Wesley posted many of his early bale-gardening success stories on our Facebook page, which is how I originally came to know him. Aren't the pictures of his farm amazing? You would guess he has been farming for many years by looking at how much production he achieves in such a small area.

## THE CONDITIONS

Wesley recalls, "I was not impressed with the soil on the farm when I moved here. It was scorched and extremely hard and lacking life. South Africa was also experiencing an epic drought at the time." Given these bleak prospects, Wesley decided to cover the ground with bales wherever there was space. Under the watchful eyes of their seven rescue dogs, Wesley and his wife would make 15 bales a day by hand. Soon they had much of their land covered. Wesley

*Top:* Straw bales placed side by side work well, but if the planting surface gets wider than 3 feet, crop shading will begin to take a toll on productivity.

*Bottom:* This garden on the dry plains of northwestern South Africa is an amazing oasis of green peppers where they simply shouldn't exist.

*Opposite:* It would have taken years and large volumes of compost to amend and add life to the existing soils where Wesley wanted to begin growing crops.

*Left:* A rudimentary structure of posts and crossbeams, made from naturally available materials, will provide much-needed shade when summer heat sets in.

*Right:* Barley, tomatoes, and peppers (pictured here) were just three of the many successful crops Bozz Man grew in his first Straw Bale Garden.

smiles as he remembers, "My wife even asked me to please leave some lawn space open for the dogs to play because I was getting carried away with making bales and had placed them wherever I could find an open spot."

As a new Straw Bale Gardener, Wesley says his biggest mistake that first year was preparing too many bales at one time. Luckily, his successful harvest of tons of vegetables was awesome. After experimenting with different techniques, Wesley discovered he prefers to place two or three bales together to make a bit more surface area for growing. "Bale gardening is really incredible," Wesley says. "I cannot think of any drawbacks to using the bale method; it works, and I am happy with the results of my bale garden."

## CROPS

Wesley's best-performing crops are tomato and chili-pepper bushes. He did some other edible trials and was impressed with the results of the barley, basil, beans, carrots, eggplant, parsley, wheat, and zucchini. Ever the researcher, Wesley is always experimenting with new tools and methods. In an unexpected outcome, the amount of compost Wesley has generated through all his bale gardening has created a huge amount of soil amendment, and his soil has truly come to life. He has started planting some crops directly into the soil because it has vastly improved after the introduction of compost. In fact, Wesley planted 30,000 sets of garlic as one cash crop this year.

## CREATING HABITAT

For Wesley, the greatest observation he made after trying Straw Bale Gardening was the thriving ecosystem created by the bale garden. He said that over a short time, he saw many different creatures and organisms move into his gardens. For the first time, he saw frogs around the garden. Spiders and snakes and birds came to eat the earthworms, which were plentiful. Mushrooms grew everywhere, and he learned about dog vomit fungus (*Fuligo septicai*) and watched it move around on several bales, though it turned out to be harmless. He observed an influx of aphids one day, and very soon after, masses of ladybug nymphs appeared along with green lacewings to go after the aphids. Wesley said, "I didn't mess with them by spraying with anything, and nature simply worked things out."

## CREATIVE SHADE

Inspired by the dead foliage underneath a palm tree, Wesley decided palm leaves would make terrific shade as a primitive cover for a handmade pergola over his vegetable garden. Acting on his idea, Wesley made wood frames and used the palm leaves over the top of large parts of his vegetable bales. In South Africa, the summer heat is very commonly 110°F, and Wesley says, "From what I have observed, one of the biggest advantages of bale gardening would be the ability to hold moisture for longer periods and the availability of nutrients." Most impressed with accumulation of worms and other life under the bales, Wesley knows his shade system has helped keep the moisture level comfortable. Without a shade system, he would need to water three times a day to stop wilting, like in any normal garden in that part of South Africa. His bales under the shade continue to thrive.

Bozz Man arrived to dry, compact, dead soil in the midst of drought. In under a year, he had turned every corner of his property green.

# A LAND-USE ANSWER IN COPENHAGEN

| NAME | |
|---|---|
| Mads Faber Henriksen/BIOARK | |
| **LOCATION** | |
| Copenhagen, Denmark | |
| **NUMBER OF BALES** | |
| 210 | |
| **CROPS** | |
| Beans, cabbage, cucumbers, herbs, peas, peppers, sunflowers, tomatoes | |
| **SBG START DATE** | |
| 2016 | |
| **CHALLENGE** | |
| Contamination and legal restrictions regarding the space for a town garden seemed insurmountable | |
| **FACEBOOK** | |
| EnergiCenter Voldparken | |

IN ORDER TO REALIZE THE DREAM of a real town garden, Mads, the director of volunteers at the EnergiCenter Voldparken (ECV) in Copenhagen, Denmark, reached out to a company called BIOARK for help. BIOARK specializes in helping restaurants, institutions, and environmentally conscious organizations implement sustainable food production for urban farms and kitchens. Mads worked closely with BIOARK CEO and founder Mikkel Stensgaard, and together they created plans to transform the entrance of EnergiCenter Voldparken.

Educated as an architect, Mikkel is always looking for new cultivation technologies and methods. Given the legal restrictions regarding land use and soil contamination on the desired site, Mikkel started passing along information about a new method for growing vegetable gardens using bales of straw. Along with innovations such as plant towers, aquaponics, and spire shelves, BIOARK's website features Straw Bale Gardens as an important solution for sustainable food production.

"The straw bales are precomposted, and the crops grow in a small layer of soil at the top of the bale. With a trellis, you can grow climbing plants such as beans. The watering can be automated. The straw bales require replacement every two years, after which the used straw bales can be composted with the kitchen waste," says Mads.

Akin to a community, cultural, or activity center, EnergiCenter Voldparken offers many facilities, programs, and services to Husum, an economically challenged urban neighborhood in Copenhagen, Denmark. More than 50 clubs and organizations use space in the

*Above:* Volunteers are key to any community-gardening project. These folks arrived on a cold day in late winter to help set up the garden.

*Opposite:* The bales are all labeled with the crops planted, so the community garden can also serve as an educational experience for all who pass by.

EnergiCenter Voldparken's Straw Bale Garden is an organic solution to sustainable food production, where they cultivate beans, salad, and herbs.

EnergiCenter Voldparken throughout the year. Offering adult and junior cooking classes, recreational sports such as gymnastics, dance, soccer, and softball, as well as disco, music, and cultural activities, EnergiCenter Voldparken provides meeting spaces, gyms, and classrooms to schools and organizations from all around Copenhagen. In fact, area kindergartens use space at the EnergiCenter Voldparken every single week.

With so much going on, Mads spends his days working with an amazing group of volunteers who make the EnergiCenter Voldparken a vibrant hub of learning, skill development, personal growth, and socialization for this Copenhagen community. As a nongardener, when Mads learned of plans for growing edibles in the space, he knew he would need to rely on outside expertise, in addition to many EnergiCenter volunteers.

It's worth noting that in Denmark, kindergartens and retirement centers have strict food standards and require 90 percent organic ingredients for all meals. Isn't that incredible? The Straw Bale Garden at EnergiCenter Voldparken meets this standard, providing fresh organic ingredients to the community-center kitchen and volunteers, as well as a local kindergarten, feeding 300 children every single day. Once a week, EnergiCenter Voldparken hosts a community meal made with garden-fresh, healthy vegetables and herbs for community

## Joel Says

Most of the population in this dense urban area of Copenhagen has little space for a traditional garden. Once the Straw Bale Garden was installed at the EnergiCenter Voldparken, it was an immediate sensation in the community. People were always stopping by to check on the progress of the garden, interested in how the plants were growing. Another advantage of creating a growing space in the middle of a community-service organization like EnergiCenter Voldparken is that its creators can now teach gardening to children, the community, and their small army of volunteers. I asked Mads if any of the folks involved in the project were skeptical about using the Straw Bale Gardens method, and he said, "Since we are located in a 'deprived urban area' with a history of vandalism, the most skepticism was about whether to establish a garden at all. A couple of environmental/urban-gardening activists did express skepticism since we did not have any experience gardening or a long-term plan."

*Above:* Mads is caught thinning a crop seeded only a few days earlier. His smile reflects the confidence that is sprouting, just as the seeds have done.

*Left:* A young volunteer helping on setup day. Kids can learn more than anyone can teach when they are immersed in something new and exciting.

A celebration al fresco in the garden, with new and old friends together enjoying fresh vegetables dotting the pies from the new outdoor pizza oven.

members—and it's totally free for senior residents. Mads says, "In the future, we hope an even larger percentage of the food for our kitchen can be grown in the garden."

One of the things the EnergiCenter Voldparken has executed so wonderfully is the incorporation of cooking classes and events in conjunction with their growing Straw Bale Gardens. From the start, chefs, kitchens, and restaurants started using Straw Bale Gardens as a way to bring new interest and customers to their tables. During the weeklong Copenhagen Cooking and Food Festival, the folks at the Organic Folkekitchen harvested vegetables directly from the bales in the town garden and enjoyed preparing meals on the grill, including pizzas topped with the harvest, and offered wine and cider from Copenhagen's cider importer.

After its first season of growing, the EnergiCenter Voldparken celebrated a successful harvest with an outdoor dinner for the community, volunteers, and staff. They enjoyed the company of guests from Norway, China, France, Italy, and Vesterbro—a hip, trendy, district of Copenhagen. The Danes are known for their *hygge*, a word that encompasses coziness and cultivating a welcoming atmosphere. In many photos of their Straw Bale Gardens, chefs guide guests through their culinary creations. In Denmark, even the Straw Bale Gardens are *hyggeligt*.

## GROWING ON OUTLAWED GROUND

Watch any video of the area surrounding the EnergiCenter Vold-parken, and you'll see visible markers of a well-worn, somewhat neglected urban space. There's graffiti, scrub and brush, concrete, lack of green space, and buildings that are in need of repair. The area sited for the Straw Bale Garden was over the space where a recreation center had been before burning to the ground after vandals set it on fire. If there was going to be a Straw Bale Garden on this land, it would be like a phoenix rising from the ashes. There were other intractable issues as well. The land was technically ownerless, yet zoning for the site did not allow for use of the soil. Furthermore, Copenhagen legally restricts using soil in urban areas to grow food due to potential soil contamination. As Mads, who had never gardened, considered this new endeavor, he feared a future of endless weeding and failed crops. Although a garden was a positive proposal for the site, in reality, it felt like an improbable dream.

Enter BIOARK, the company founded by Mikkel Stensgaard, who has a special gift for bringing urban farms to unlikely areas all over Copenhagen. Aware of a constellation of progressive solutions in sustainable food production, Mikkel felt Straw Bale Gardening was the perfect solution for the site. To prepare the site, landscape fabric would be laid over the land, not to prevent weeds but rather to prevent the plants growing in the bales from rooting into the ground. Mikkel designed a robust garden based on a plan that included 210 bales. In their marketing materials, Danes proudly call the garden at EnergiCenter Voldparken "perhaps the largest Straw Bale Garden in the world."

Sourcing all the bales from a local farmer, the garden was set up quickly on the Planting Day, or "Plantedag," on April 30, 2016. Despite the cold (everyone was wearing winter coats, hats, and mittens), volunteers from all over Copenhagen showed up to set the bales in place. To prevent any late-spring frost damage, trellises were placed above the bales to support plastic sheeting that could be pulled over the earliest plantings on cold nights. Young and old, experienced gardeners and newbies worked together to string the wire between the trellis posts. Right next to the garden, volunteers added sticks and organic material to the large insect hotel made with recycled pallets. When the setup was complete, the volunteers enjoyed wood-fired pizzas with fresh ingredients—some volunteers even brought edible flowers and herbs for the pesto, pizza, and salad.

The conditioning and bale preparation were completed by Mads and his army of volunteers. Overcoming legalities and a small budget, the garden became a reality. Today, the EnergiCenter Voldparken

### Joel Says

In this case, Mikkel placed landscape fabric on top of the soil to act as a barrier between the bales and the soil beneath the fabric. Plants in bales are pretty happy. Happy plants have happy, vigorous root systems. It's not uncommon for the plants in bales to root themselves through the bale and into the soil. This is not an issue unless there is a concern about soil contamination. In the case of the EnergiCenter Voldparken garden, fears of soil contamination meant that the plants needed to be thwarted from rooting into the soil. Double and sometimes triple layering landscape fabric can be necessary to prevent roots from doing what they do best: finding a way to make contact with the earth.

## Joel Says

It would be my dream one day to have community gardens installed adjacent to every major residential building complex or wherever a temporary space was available in every major city. This could allow people to do a bit of gardening without having to own land, buy tools, or spend much time pulling weeds or remembering to water. A garden like this one in Denmark would be easy to scale to a much larger size or smaller size, with just enough bales to fit into the space available. Straw Bale Gardening is very predictable, while unfamiliar soils (or even familiar soils) are impossible to predict. If we started with a consistent bale of straw and used the same conditioning process, watered using the same basic formula, and planted the same seeds each year, the only remaining factor is the sun, and the outcome would be extremely consistent. Removing variables and eliminating unpredictable outcomes is key to scaling any project like this.

garden boasts chicken and rabbit farms, a vegetable, fruit, and herb garden, a lush greenhouse, and a strawberry garden. The bales and the animals are a draw for visitors who casually socialize in the space. Serving two purposes, production and education, the Straw Bale Garden is also used as a venue for events for companies and private parties. An outdoor kitchen, complete with a pizza oven, makes the garden an extra-special venue.

Besides serving the area's residents, EnergiCenter Voldparken is committed to helping the onsite kitchen with fresh vegetables, fruits, and herbs. Every day, chef Martin Pihl prepares meals for 300 kindergarten children, and the satisfaction of using fresh, organic ingredients is a source of endless inspiration. Chef Pihl especially enjoys using fresh strawberries from the strawberry bales. He is also fond of making salads, and rhubarb is a Danish favorite.

### CROPS

The EnergiCenter Voldparken garden was planted with a bit of everything because it was serving as an educational garden in addition to a production garden. Crops that create a large vine field were avoided because the center needed to keep the garden neat, as children and families would be walking around the area. Tomatoes, potatoes, cucumbers, cabbage, beets, leeks, kale, lettuce, chard, basil, thyme, parsley, chives, oregano, and many other herbs were selected for the first crops. Weekly meals were served outdoors during the summers, and people were seated around long farm tables right out by the garden. Mads says, "This urban garden has had an amazing calming effect on the people involved and on the whole neighborhood." One key indication of the value placed on the garden is that it has never been vandalized.

*Opposite, top:* With contaminated soils, cover the soil with ground cloth and position the bales on top to prevent any plant roots from getting to the soil.

*Opposite, bottom:* Neighbors will ask if you're building a go-kart track or bringing in goats, but once they learn the basics, they usually hop on the bale wagon.

Executive chef Paul Lynch spearheaded a Straw Bale Garden project at the Hyatt Regency in Bloomington, Minnesota, for his Urbana Craft Kitchen and Market Restaurant.

# CHAPTER 6

# FUTURE SOLUTIONS

## The Future of Straw Bale Gardening and Resources to Help a New Straw Bale Gardener

SINCE 2009, THE YEAR WHEN I DRAFTED and began distributing my first self-published booklet with the details about the method, I estimate that the number of people growing their own vegetable gardens in bales grows by a factor of five times each year, at least. Have a conversation with anyone who has grown their garden in bales already, and it will explain this phenomenon. Every Straw Bale Gardener ends up being approached by skeptics, neighbors, and friends who ask questions about this unusual garden and then get sucked into how simple and successful it is. They end up excitedly sharing the idea and supporting five new gardeners the next year, and then those five friends each support five more new converts to the Straw Bale Gardens technique. It's kind of like a pyramid scheme, except there isn't a scheme, and nobody makes money from this pyramid. It wouldn't be logical to assume that the Straw Bale Gardens method would continue to grow at the fast pace that it has grown over the past few years, but I sure hope it does. It certainly doesn't seem to be slowing down yet. Is it possible that for those who said it's a "fad" 24 years ago when I started doing it would still be in the dark about all the benefits of using this method? I have had my share of skeptics through the years, but the proof is now indisputable.

The Straw Bale Gardens method continues to grow in popularity around the United States, Canada, and around much of western Europe as well, which is wonderful. I am most excited, however, about what is happening in Asia, Africa, and South America, where some of the world's poorest populations exist. They have little knowledge of gardening to rely upon. They do not own land or tools, and they have meager resources for investing in a garden or raised beds. Their climate is often difficult to grow in, with soggy soil due to excessive rain or drought. Bales, however, are very inexpensive, even free if made by hand, and the preparation can be done for little or no cost as well. The bales require no tools and can grow many varieties of vegetables and fruits essential to the diet of people all over the world. The bales drain excessive moisture quickly and hold water well for dry periods. The bales take up little space and can go anywhere—on concrete, asphalt, or any soil, even contaminated soil—without adverse effects. They can be placed close to the front door or on a rooftop so the owner can keep an eye on their crops.

Are straw bales the answer, or even the beginning of the answer, to urban food security issues happening in cities around the world? I don't know, but I think the Straw Bale Gardens technique has a shot at filling the hungry stomachs of people all around the world. We have proof that it works, and we have momentum, so now all we need is some movement. Can you help? Yes, you can help, by spreading the word, talking about your experience online, and encouraging anyone you know who could benefit from having a garden at home to try it. Support them with your experience and show them how it works. They will look back and have you to thank in a few years when their Straw Bale Garden becomes an important part of their life.

There are many resources that a new Straw Bale Gardener can turn to for help in getting started. Here are a few.

***Straw Bale Gardens Complete.*** This is my first published book, which was released as a second edition with additional information about organic techniques, water conservation, and making bales yourself, along with other additional information for readers. The book is very well illustrated and has detailed step-by-step instructions for conditioning bales, finding the correct fertilizer to use, setting up the water system, setting up the trellis system, managing insects and diseases, and many other tips and tricks. The book also has a detailed glossary of vegetables with specific Straw Bale Gardening–related information. I am very proud to say that the book has become the standard bearer for the Straw Bale Gardens technique. I would encourage anyone growing a Straw Bale Garden to have a copy of it on your shelf; it is a must-have reference to answer the questions that many new growers haven't thought of yet! The book is available in several foreign languages as well, so if you have a friend in another country, look for the translation and get them a copy as well.

**The Straw Bale Gardens App.** Our app can be downloaded for free from the Apple App Store, Google Play, or other app store on your device. The app is made to work on any type of mobile device. The app is a great way to watch video testimonials and how-to videos on many different Straw Bale Gardening–related subjects. You can also find a calendar of events where I am speaking around the country and world. If you see anything nearby, please come say hi. I love to meet people who are using the Straw Bale Gardens method or who are considering using it.

**www.StrawBaleMarket.com.** This is a website that is owned and run by me for free to all users. It is designed to allow people to search by ZIP code or on our map for suppliers of straw bales for gardening or to sell straw bales. It is completely free to access and use whether using it for buying or selling bales. We do require that you register to use the website, but that is only because we try to keep spammers from making fake posts on the website. We do not use any of the data collected on that website for marketing or sales.

**www.StrawBaleGardens.com.** This is is the main website where folks can learn about the Straw Bale Gardens methods, my books, and other products offered for sale. In addition, there is an extensive photo gallery of gardens, other information about upcoming events, and my biographical info. There is a media page with links to many of our past newspaper and magazine articles and radio and TV appearances. You can also register for upcoming webinars or link to many other Straw Bale Gardening–related pages, including a link to my blog.

**The Certified Straw Bale Gardening Instructor program, www.StrawBaleGardens.com/directory.** Over the years, many individuals asked me to come to speak at their garden club or their event, which I often do. The problem arises when travel expenses start to make it difficult for everyone. The solution was to take those who have become big fans of the Straw Bale Gardens method and give them assistance and minor training to become presenters themselves so they can teach seminars and give classes. From this idea was born the Certified Straw Bale Gardening Instructors program, which now has well over 100 instructors enrolled from all around the world. The program is helpful for those planning to give a presentation, because we provide PowerPoint slide presentations, posters, flyers, sample speaking contracts and press releases, and other tools to make whatever event the speaker is doing a success. It is free to join as of this writing, so if anyone with experience growing a Straw Bale Garden is interested in becoming an instructor, please get in touch on the website, and we can provide you with the details.

**My blog, www.strawbalegardens.com/blog.** My blog is a great place to go to read about many aspects of Straw Bale Gardening that you may have trouble finding from any other source. Many of the blog entries actually started as answers to common questions people have, and the blog allows me to get into much greater detail than I would have time to write in my answer to a question posted online or emailed. If you ever send in a question, please be aware that I may simply link you over to my blog to a post where your question is answered thoroughly. It isn't that I don't want to answer every question individually, but it can be difficult when I get hundreds of them (many times the same questions) from people around the world each day, especially in the spring.

**www.StrawBaleGardenClub.com.** If you are a person who likes to see someone visually demonstrate things rather than just reading about the techniques in a book, then the Straw Bale Garden Club might be the perfect resource for you. If you visit the site, you will see a directory with around 100 different Straw Bale Gardening videos that cover almost every different subject. From bale preparation to fertilizing and watering to harvesting and cleanup, you will find a video on every subject. These videos are all shot in high definition with professional audio, so they are well done, and the solid advice is based on tons of experience and study.

**Straw Bale Garden Facebook group, www.facebook.com/ LearnToGrowAStrawBaleGarden.** I understand that Facebook is not for everyone—but if you *are* a user, please check out our page. You might also search for other Straw Bale Garden pages and groups; there are over 100 from many different states and countries, and some are focused only on organic while others are about high elevations or desert climates. There are several Straw Bale Gardening pages in different languages as well, so if English isn't your first language, you can find a home with another group or page.

**Bale Buster.** This is a brand-new product I've spent 3 years developing and am now marketing. It is a natural bale-conditioning agent that makes the bale-preparation process very easy for anyone. It is 100 percent organic, but the cost is much more economical than any other comparable organic, high-nitrogen, protein-based product on the market today. Bale Buster contains a protein-based nitrogen source and an inoculation of shelf-stable bacteria and fungi, which will help with the conditioning process of the bales. Using Bale Buster will speed the conditioning process and ensure that the bales are ready to plant quickly and naturally. Check our website for more details about the product and to find retail locations where Bale Buster is sold.

**Social media.** Gardeners tend to love sharing pictures and asking for advice using many forms of social media. Along with Facebook, I also use the sites below.

Instagram: @strawbalegarden

Twitter: @strawbalegarden

LinkedIn: Straw Bale Gardens (group)

Tumblr: StrawBaleGardens

Facebook: www.facebook.com/LearnToGrowAStrawBaleGarden

# RESOURCE GUIDE

**Straw Bale Gardens**
www.StrawBaleGardens.com

**Joel's blog, common questions and answers**
www.StrawBaleGardens.com/blog

**Free marketplace to buy or sell straw bales**
www.StrawBaleMarket.com

**Make your own hand baler video**
www.youtube.com/watch?v=c_dYfTc1Wsc

**Straw Bale Gardens Complete**
www.StrawBaleGardens.com/Store

**Join the online Straw Bale Gardening community**
www.StrawBaleGardenClub.com

**International Garden Festival in France**
www.domaine-chaumont.fr/en/international-garden-festival

**Joel's main Facebook Page**
www.Facebook.com/LearnToGrowAStrawBaleGarden

**Joel's list of events and appearances**
www.strawbalegardens.com/speaking-engagements/seminars-classes

**BaleBuster™ organic bale conditioner**
www.StrawBaleGardens.com/Store

# METRIC CONVERSIONS

## METRIC EQUIVALENT

| | 1/64 | 1/32 | 1/25 | 1/16 | 1/8 | 1/4 | 3/8 | 2/5 | 1/2 | 5/8 | 3/4 | 7/8 | 1 | 2 | 3 | 4 | 5 | 6 | 7 | 8 | 9 | 10 | 11 | 12 | 36 | 39.4 |
|---|---|---|---|---|---|---|---|---|---|---|---|---|---|---|---|---|---|---|---|---|---|---|---|---|---|---|
| Inches (in.) | 1/64 | 1/32 | 1/25 | 1/16 | 1/8 | 1/4 | 3/8 | 2/5 | 1/2 | 5/8 | 3/4 | 7/8 | 1 | 2 | 3 | 4 | 5 | 6 | 7 | 8 | 9 | 10 | 11 | 12 | 36 | 39.4 |
| Feet (ft.) | | | | | | | | | | | | | | | | | | | | | | | | 1 | 3 | 3 1/12 |
| Yards (yd.) | | | | | | | | | | | | | | | | | | | | | | | | | 1 | 1 1/12 |
| Millimeters (mm) | 0.40 | 0.79 | 1 | 1.59 | 3.18 | 6.35 | 9.53 | 10 | 12.7 | 15.9 | 19.1 | 22.2 | 25.4 | 50.8 | 76.2 | 101.6 | 127 | 152 | 178 | 203 | 229 | 254 | 279 | 305 | 914 | 1,000 |
| Centimeters (cm) | | | | | | | 0.95 | 1 | 1.27 | 1.59 | 1.91 | 2.22 | 2.54 | 5.08 | 7.62 | 10.16 | 12.7 | 15.2 | 17.8 | 20.3 | 22.9 | 25.4 | 27.9 | 30.5 | 91.4 | 100 |
| Meters (m) | | | | | | | | | | | | | | | | | | | | | | | | .30 | .91 | 1.00 |

## CONVERTING MEASUREMENTS

| TO CONVERT: | TO: | MULTIPLY BY: |
|---|---|---|
| Inches | Millimeters | 25.4 |
| Inches | Centimeters | 2.54 |
| Feet | Meters | 0.305 |
| Yards | Meters | 0.914 |
| Miles | Kilometers | 1.609 |
| Square inches | Square centimeters | 6.45 |
| Square feet | Square meters | 0.093 |
| Square yards | Square meters | 0.836 |
| Cubic inches | Cubic centimeters | 16.4 |
| Cubic feet | Cubic meters | 0.0283 |
| Cubic yards | Cubic meters | 0.765 |
| Pints (U.S.) | Liters | 0.473 (Imp. 0.568) |
| Quarts (U.S.) | Liters | 0.946 (Imp. 1.136) |
| Gallons (U.S.) | Liters | 3.785 (Imp. 4.546) |
| Ounces | Grams | 28.4 |
| Pounds | Kilograms | 0.454 |
| Tons | Metric tons | 0.907 |

| TO CONVERT: | TO: | MULTIPLY BY: |
|---|---|---|
| Millimeters | Inches | 0.039 |
| Centimeters | Inches | 0.394 |
| Meters | Feet | 3.28 |
| Meters | Yards | 1.09 |
| Kilometers | Miles | 0.621 |
| Square centimeters | Square inches | 0.155 |
| Square meters | Square feet | 10.8 |
| Square meters | Square yards | 1.2 |
| Cubic centimeters | Cubic inches | 0.061 |
| Cubic meters | Cubic feet | 35.3 |
| Cubic meters | Cubic yards | 1.31 |
| Liters | Pints (U.S.) | 2.114 (Imp. 1.76) |
| Liters | Quarts (U.S.) | 1.057 (Imp. 0.88) |
| Liters | Gallons (U.S.) | 0.264 (Imp. 0.22) |
| Grams | Ounces | 0.035 |
| Kilograms | Pounds | 2.2 |
| Metric tons | Tons | 1.1 |

## CONVERTING TEMPERATURES

Convert degrees Fahrenheit (F) to degrees Celsius (C) by following this simple formula: Subtract 32 from the Fahrenheit temperature reading. Then mulitply that number by 5/9. For example, 77°F - 32 = 45. 45 × 5/9 = 25°C.

To convert degrees Celsius to degrees Fahrenheit, multiply the Celsius temperature reading by 9/5, then add 32. For example, 25°C × 9/5 = 45. 45 + 32 = 77°F.

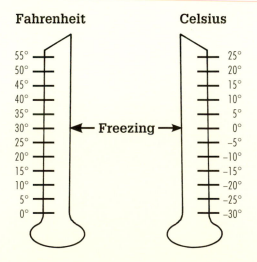

# PHOTO CREDITS

# INDEX

# MEET JOEL KARSTEN

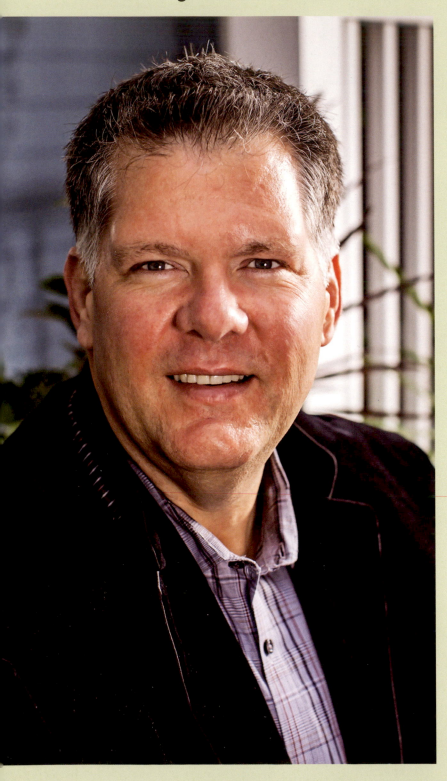

JOEL KARSTEN, a farm boy who grew up tending a soil garden like other gardeners have for centuries, shook up the gardening world with his first book describing his breakthrough Straw Bale Gardening concept. The *New York Times* called Straw Bale Gardening "a revolutionary gardening method," and his ideas have been enthusiastically embraced globally, making his books best-sellers in many languages. Karsten earned a BS in horticulture from the University of Minnesota and spends his summers tending his vegetable garden, doing research, and experimenting with new ideas and methods he can pass along to his followers. He is a popular speaker, making appearances around the world at events that celebrate innovation, garden enthusiasts, and healthful lifestyles, and he is renowned for his social-media presence, blog, and impressions. Karsten has inspired tens of thousands of first-time gardeners and a legion of "seasoned" growers who found a new and better way to pursue their passion, as well as enabled "retired" gardeners to begin gardening again since his method eliminates the physical challenges found in traditional soil gardening. Discover more information about Karsten and his revolutionary methods at www.StrawBaleGardens.com. Links to his Facebook page, WordPress blog, YouTube channel, Twitter, and Google Plus can all be found on his website.